We HAVE A SECRET

BY
HELENA VILAR

Conscious Dreams
PUBLISHING

We Have a Secret

Copyright © 2024: Helena Vilar

All rights reserved. No part of this publication may be produced, distributed, or transmitted in any form or by any means, including photocopying, recording, or other electronic or mechanical methods, without the prior written permission of the publisher, except in the case of brief quotations embodied in critical reviews and certain other non-commercial uses permitted by copyright law.

I have tried to recreate events, locales and conversations from my memories of them. In order to maintain their anonymity in some instances I have changed the names of individuals and places, I may have changed some identifying characteristics and details such as physical properties, occupations and places of residence.

Published by Conscious Dreams Publishing
www.consciousdreamspublishing.com

Edited by Daniella Blechner and Elise Abram
Typeset and ebook formatting by: Amit Dey
Cover Designed by Emily's World of Design

ISBN: 978-1-915522-91-7

DEDICATION

This book is dedicated to my children. It should be to my beloved husband, but he's not present to see this dedication. I'm proud to say that I have four wonderful and strong children. They had good times with their parents. They saw my joy and my sadness and were always ready to give me love and support.

Continue to be strong to face this world we live in. May God protect you always. Your father is always watching over you.

Thank you, Catarina, Jessica, João Carlos and Camilla.

CONTENTS

Introduction vii
Author's Note ix
Chapter 1: Love 1
Chapter 2: The Beginning 7
Chapter 3: The Pain 15
Chapter 4: Faith 23
Chapter 5: Telling My Family 29
Chapter 6: Great Expectation 35
Chapter 7: Bring the Pain 43
Chapter 8: Creator. 49
Chapter 9: Torn into Pieces 59
Chapter 10: False Hope 65
Chapter 11: Broken 69
Chapter 12: Time After Time 77

Chapter 13: Losing My Mind 81

Chapter 14: Losing the Power to Walk. 89

Chapter 15: Hallucination 95

Chapter 16: The Road to the End 99

Chapter 17: Goodbye 105

Chapter 18: The End of our Beautiful Love Story . . .113

Epilogue 121

Torn Pieces of Me 121

My Daughter Camilla's Chapter 129

INTRODUCTION

Welcome to 'We Have a Secret.'
Before you dive into this book, I have to say that everything that I've written has been my life experience. I started writing this book with my husband. Whenever something happened, I made sure I was careful to write it down. There were many times my husband was lying on the sofa very sick. When I looked at him, something inside of me awakened my inner being and gave me the strength to write. I'm writing so everyone knows our story. I hope I can help someone who is going through the same thing right now.

AUTHOR'S NOTE

My name is Helena. I was born in Angola to a very big family. My mother had six children: two boys and four girls. At nine months old, we left Angola and went to São Tomé and Príncipe, my mother's home country. I ended up leaving São Tomé at the age of six, so I could live with my father in Angola, as my parents were separated. About two years ago, I went to be with my mother and siblings again. We ended up migrating to Portugal when I was around ten years old, and that is where I grew up. It was in Portugal that I became a dreamer, and I've made many of those dreams come true. I fantasised about growing up and having a good job, meeting an amazing husband, and having a house with many children running around, and they all came true, but I never expected this to be my reality. I have always been a person who dreams a lot, and whilst many manifested, there are a few I still need to tick off, including writing a book. But if you are reading this, it means I made another dream come true.

In life, I faced many hardships. I didn't have an easy upbringing, but it wasn't too bad, either. I was grateful to always have some form of roof over my head, but that isn't the premise of this book. In fact, when I thought about writing a book, I wanted it to be about love. I had a few boyfriends before meeting João, but I did not know what love meant until I met him.

Today, I'm sharing with you how my life has changed, and how in three years, all of my dreams were put on pause, how my life as a simple mother and wife changed to be the wife of a man with a chronic illness. As I said, I have four children, and in my family, we talk about everything openly with each other, except this.

CHAPTER 1

LOVE

Several of you already know our secret, but many others are still unaware of what goes on behind closed doors. Let us take this journey together to get to know the VilarFamily better and what we have endured over the past three years. I am a mother of four and a wife. I have been blessed with my eldest children — Catarina (24) and Jessica (21) and my youngest — João Carlos (12) and Camilla (11).

Today, many people know us as the VilarFamily. Through social media, we have interacted with thousands of followers, and we could not be more grateful. These are opportunities I never thought I would have. I was born in Angola and raised in Portugal, which is where I met the love of my life, my husband João.

We met all the way back in 1996 whilst I was working. When I met João, I was 18 or 19 years old. I was living in student accommodation, and I worked at night to help myself with my studies and with the house. I worked in a bar, and one day as I was making a drink for someone, I saw João and his friend standing near the counter. I approached them and introduced myself. João turned around and gave me a smile. What a smile! It was one of the most beautiful smiles I'd ever seen. I asked God to never forget this smile. And what I'm going to say now is the pure truth. From the day I met João until today, I have never forgotten the way he turned to see me. He turned with a smile. I don't think I ever want to forget it.

I gave them a table and noticed João kept looking at me. I looked at him, too. He was a very handsome boy, and he had good energy. That day had passed, and nothing happened between us. When I saw him for the first time, I didn't look at him with a passionate look. I just thought he was very handsome, and I liked his energy. When I met him, I had a boyfriend. I was dating someone my mother didn't approve of because he was much older than me. My boyfriend and I were about 15 years apart. João and I became friends and exchanged telephone numbers — my home phone because mobile phones didn't exist then. João always called me, and I didn't want to answer so my mother spoke to him. One day my mother said, 'I don't know why you don't stay with this boy who always calls you; he seems like a good guy.'

A couple of weeks went by and João returned to the bar. At this point, I was no longer dating. We had a conversation, and I asked him if he had a girlfriend. He said 'no'. I asked him if I could compete to be his girlfriend and he said 'yes'.

We started going out, and I told him, 'Don't fall in love please. Let's just play and then we'll see what happens.'

A month passed, and we were still together. We were in the car talking and he told me that the first time he saw me, he told his friend, 'I'm going to make love to this beautiful girl.'

I was shocked by his sincerity with me. I asked him, 'When you tried this beautiful girl, why didn't you leave? He said he wanted to try it again.

This blossoming relationship resulted in 25 years of much love, respect and four beautiful children. Today I know that I fell in love with him from the first day I saw him, and I still won't forget his smile or the way he turned to see me. Today I can admit that it was love at first sight. Our destiny was set on this day.

When João met me. He lied about his age. He said he was younger because he knew I was younger. He told me he was three years younger. I told him that I always liked older men. After months of being together, I found out he was seven years older than me. This difference has never been a problem for me.

Years later, I still listen to a song called 'Next to You' by Justin Bieber and Chris Brown. When I first heard the lyrics, I screamed and said to my kids, 'This is my song! All I ask God for is for me to not forget about your daddy's smile whenever I hear this song.

Two of our children were born in London, and the other two were born in Portugal. We emigrated from Portugal to provide a better life for our kids, which we did.

Like everyone else who flees their home nation in the quest for a better life, we landed in England. We have always been the VilarFamily, even before it became our brand on social media. We have always been a typical, modest household; nothing false exists within it, and we transmit all the happiness and free-spirited energy we possess.

My family means the world to me, and that goes for my husband, too. It was always his dream to be a father, and he is the best I could have hoped for.

2018 was a hard year, full of changes and battles we had to endure. I was working at a local grocery store in their bakery, making cakes and pastries and talking to customers, which I enjoyed, but I was given a job opportunity that would pay three times more than what I was making at the grocery store. I told myself that I had to do it, so I quit the job I liked—where all the staff knew me, and I got along well with everyone—to start a new job, something challenging. I went on to do a web developer course, but I had not even finished it before I began my new role. When I did, it was completely unrelated to what I had in mind, and I experienced a lot of hardship. I enjoy communicating with people and helping, which is why I felt my expectation for the new role had not been met, even though my employers were decent people. I had to finish the course while working there because I had already started it. It was advantageous because I could do both at once, and I was making a fine living.

João and I planned a trip to Amsterdam with some friends in October 2018. There were six of us in total. We took our car—a seven-seater—because we wanted to drive there. While driving, João complained of back pains and aches in his bottom. He suffered with anguish when we got to Amsterdam. We got him painkillers. We walked anywhere we could go because he was still in pain, and the medicine did not make it go away. We went to a party in Amsterdam at night, but because João was in so much pain, we had to leave. Even on the day of our trip back home, João was in a lot of discomfort, but he still managed to drive the entire distance.

When we got back to London, I was at work when João called me to say that he could not handle the pain any longer, so I advised him to go to the hospital because the GP would only write off his pain with a painkiller. He could not drive himself because of the pain, so my eldest daughter drove him to the hospital. He'd had diarrhoea for three months, of which I was unaware because he had not mentioned it to me, and when he got to the hospital, he was told to do a colonoscopy.

One day in November, my daughter walked into the room to see her father and found him sobbing. Her heart dropped when she realised they had taken some tissue for a biopsy.

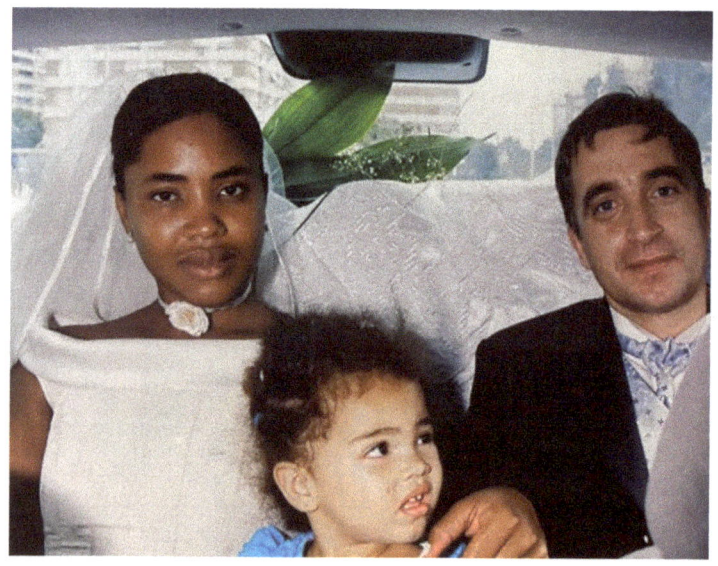

CHAPTER 2

THE BEGINNING

João enjoyed driving, and he knew London quite well, so he quit his job to become an Uber driver. Whilst studying for this, we awaited the biopsy results. It played on his mind; as the intelligent man he was, he never stopped researching his symptoms and what might be causing them.

One day, he came to me to say that he believed it to be cancer. My heart broke, and I pleaded with him not to say or even think of such things, but a part of me panicked. I put on a brave face, even though I believed it could be cancer.

On a random Thursday, 13 December 2018, the doctor called to let us know he had the results of the biopsy. I told my employers about what was going on with my husband and that I had to accompany him to the hospital. I was quite anxious to learn the outcome on the day of the meeting since, in my mind, if it were not serious, they would not have scheduled an appointment to inform us of the outcome. I panicked, but I couldn't show my family that I was panicking.

My husband and I arrived at the doctor's office after they called us, along with my oldest daughter. The doctor explained the cause of my husband's pain, and then he uttered the word I was least prepared to hear. Cancer. That word is only ever used in movies, on television, and with other people; it was never used in our family or with someone we loved.

As soon as the doctor stated, 'João, you have cancer,' everything came crashing down on me at that point, and I was floored. I looked at my daughter, who was already crying, and then at João who was remarkably composed. I tried to look inward to see how I was doing, but it was impossible because I was cold and my body was immobile.

I couldn't believe what the doctor had told us. It wasn't true. It couldn't be true.

I started crying.

The doctor informed João that he had bowel cancer, and it was large, but further tests needed to be done to determine if it had spread to other parts of his body.

Leaving the hospital with this news was challenging. I hugged my husband tighter than I had before and assured him that everything would be okay, but he told me he had been mentally preparing for this news.

My eldest daughter could only shiver.

My daughter, Jessica, had no clue. She was highly intelligent and in the process of completing her entrance exams for university. When all of this happened, she was attending a residential at Oxford University to get acquainted with the environment, but she wasn't a fan. She also had an interview scheduled for Cambridge University, and we wanted her to do her best. We knew the news would break her, so we waited until she got home from school to break the news to her. She couldn't stop crying. It was a devastating period in all of our lives

We loved Christmas, and it was quickly approaching. We had many people coming to celebrate with us, including my niece, Jandira, who purchased plane tickets for the occasion. She came with her daughters and her husband, as well as a niece of mine, who was already residing with us. Her sister had also come from Portugal. My house would be quite crowded because my uncle also came to spend Christmas with us, along with his wife and seven children. I wondered how I was going to manage because I could not cancel, but I also didn't want to talk to anyone about what we were going through.

We discussed our options and decided against postponing Christmas, even though we were suffering badly. It started to affect us physically and emotionally. Jessica attended her Cambridge interview, but due to her nerves and emotions, she did not get in despite her amazing grades.

That was when it hit.

Christmas came. The house was packed. Although we had an incredibly fantastic Christmas, we cried every night before bed. We normally enjoyed having guests over, but given the circumstances, I wished the celebrations had ended sooner.

I was on vacation from work, and when my vacation was over, I had to return. When I got to the office, though, my managers weren't there, so I worked by myself all the time, and I had no idea what was ahead. When my managers visited the office to speak with me one day, they told me that I would have to close the office permanently because the person they were working for had not paid them, leaving me with little choice but to shut down the company.

From what I heard, my life was about to come to a halt. I had lost my job, and my husband couldn't work, so we had no income. On top of that, the love of my life had cancer. The bad news just felt like it was piling on and more came each week, like a cycle of pain, and it was too much for us to handle, but I knew I had to have the courage for my family. There were five individuals who relied on me.

How would I survive without a job? How would we survive? How could I even think of a job when my husband needed me the most? We knew we had to save money since unexpected expenses would inevitably arise—something I can't recommend enough is to have emergency savings because life is not easy, nor is it fair.

The best part of this was that I had a highly intelligent husband who constantly considered the future. What helped us was that João has always enjoyed saving money and thank God it was what he'd amassed that supported us in our time of greatest need.

Having to deal with so much negative news had already worn me out, and it continued when my eldest daughter also lost her job.

We hadn't discussed the news much since receiving it, but now that the parties were over, the house was silent, and we knew as we waited for further results. João had another appointment on 27 December when he was informed that the cancer had spread to his liver.

The month of January 2019 was very hard for us. Our rooms were dark, and the house felt cold. João did not want to get out of bed. He was suffering, and I felt hopeless.

One day, I left the house to go shopping alone, hoping to relieve some stress, but all I found myself doing was crying about everything that had happened. I remember telling myself that I could not let the news end my family and everything we had built. I felt the need to do something for our family, so we didn't fall into a bottomless pit of despair. I remember coming home with sushi for my husband because I knew he loved it. I opened all of the curtains and windows to get some fresh air into the house and managed to breathe a little.

One thing I often do in my house is hold meetings in which we talk about what's happening around the house and how we can solve it, and that's exactly what we did. We sat our two eldest daughters down in the living room. I remember us telling them there was no denying that what we were going through was horrible, but we had to live our lives and not our problems. We wanted to reassure them that the news didn't mean their father was going anywhere or that he would stop being the João we always knew.

It felt like a weight was lifted from João's shoulders, knowing he had all of our love and support. The next day, he was out of bed and back into the routine of making breakfast for the younger ones and taking them to school.

CHAPTER 3

THE PAIN

The hospital appointments continued. We had more consultations with the doctor who had diagnosed him and another with the liver doctor. This time, all four of us went—my husband and I, along with my eldest daughters—with the hope that we would be told he was in stage two and solutions were available.

We were hit with more pain when we got to the appointment—not only had the cancer spread to three areas of his body (liver, lungs, and bowel), but he was also in stage four. At that point, the room became silent, and any hope we walked in with was left in that hospital room.

The urgency kept piling up when João was booked for his first bowel operation, having decided it would be too risky to operate on his liver and lungs, igniting some hope that something was possible. His operation was scheduled at Royal London Hospital. It felt like the longest journey. We drove all the way there in complete silence.

As soon as we parked the car, it felt as if a switch had been flipped, and all the air was sucked out. I had a panic attack. It felt like a ball was stuck in my throat that would not let me breathe or scream. It spread to my legs, and I froze in fear. I remember someone walking through the car park, asking if I was doing okay and if I needed any help, and a voice responding with, 'She will be okay. I am helping her.' My daughter Jessica—the one I usually help with panic attacks—was now comforting her mother, helping her through her panic attack, helping her breathe. That day went by in a blur. It was spent crying and praying.

At home, I had no clue what to do with myself. I had no job since my bosses had to close the office due to financial issues, and there wasn't much I could do to help my husband if it wasn't for tending to him to make him comfortable. Now that I look back on it, I feel as though my employers lied about the whole financial debacle. I had only worked with them for about three months when I told them about my husband. They knew I would need some time off and that I would be of no use to them. It's sad to think of how humans operate and think, even when they know their actions may ruin someone else's life.

It was difficult to process everything, especially since we never told anyone what was going on out of respect for my husband, who did not want anyone to worry about him. Pretending everything was okay was exhausting, and it went on for another three months. I wished I could talk to someone about what we were going through because João suffered in silence and didn't want to talk about it as the subject made him sad, but I felt as if I was suffocating. I felt as though I'd stopped talking to everyone for three months. I would put on a happy face for Instagram, wish everyone a good morning, tell them what I had planned for the day with a smile, and put my phone down before being thrown back into reality.

I knew I needed someone, so I reached out to a dear friend and neighbour, Jessica, who had a church and whose husband was a pastor. We had known each other for a while, as her daughter was best friends with my daughter Camilla. I told her about the situation, and they asked if they could come to our home to say a prayer for João and the family. João accepted, and that day, Jessica and her husband, Frank, said a heartfelt prayer for us. It felt like all we had available to us was our faith.

I called another friend, Laudilena—someone we had known since we moved to London and another strong believer of Christ—and told her about the situation, but I said the situation was happening to a friend of ours and not João so as not to worry her. Her words soothed me. She said, 'Helena, with God, nothing is impossible. I believe my God is powerful and compassionate and capable of healing.' It was as if she knew exactly what I needed to hear.

Whilst this was all happening, our friends from Poland organised a party with all of our friends and wanted us to come. João was not mentally ready to be around people, but I convinced him, telling him it would be good for him to leave the house and spend some time with his friends, the same group we had gone to Amsterdam with. They were aware of the pain he was in and that he had done some tests. My dear friend, who I considered family, kept asking questions as she could tell I wasn't doing too well, but I couldn't bring myself to tell her, either. It felt like a private matter, something only we should know, so I told her what I had been telling everyone: 'Everything is okay.'

At the party, we ate, talked and even danced a little. João didn't initially want to drink, but he had one cup of red wine throughout the night, and it felt good to see him enjoy a little. I indulged a little more than João, so I was already feeling a little dizzy from the drink, but I saw João leave the table to sit on the sofa, so I followed him. I barely had the time to sit down before he started vomiting everywhere.

Anyone who knows me knows that I hate vomit, but for my husband, I grabbed as much of the vomit as I could, and my friend came running over with a bag to help me. It was all over the sofa, so I helped clean everything up, and João lay down to get some rest so we could go home.

My friend, who I considered family, was already suspicious, but she didn't say anything. She cleaned up and went outside to smoke, and I followed her for some fresh air. It was me, her, and another friend. I wasn't as close to the other woman as it was a new friendship, and she didn't know my family or our situation that well, but at that moment, it didn't matter.

My throat closed up, and I felt another panic attack coming on. All I remember was screaming, 'My husband has cancer!'

My friend and I burst into tears. All she could do was hug me whilst I felt my world crumbling. I know I yelled, which meant João, who was inside with his friends, also heard. Everyone came running and tried to comfort us, telling us to stop crying and come back in.

All I could do was look at my husband, thinking it was best to go home. It felt like a lot had happened in a few hours. My friends had found out this horrible news in what was meant to be a happy moment, my husband had thrown up, and I had revealed a secret I wasn't meant to. I felt so bad telling everyone something João had asked me not to, but he wasn't mad because he knew how badly I felt and how alone I was with no one to talk to. I didn't know how to talk to my friend. She was my best friend. We talked about everything, but I kept this secret from her. I was afraid to call her.

My friend messaged me the next day, expressing how sorry she was over the news of João's illness. She gave us her support, and we felt a little better knowing we had people in our corner who also had hope. Meanwhile, we still hadn't told any of our families, and we knew that would be the next hardest thing to do.

CHAPTER 4

FAITH

We had another consultation, talking us through the operation and any complications we might face. My husband attended, along with Catarina and her boyfriend. It was the first time a stoma—an opening made through the abdominal wall and connecting to the bowel—was mentioned, meaning that João would need a disposable bag to store his stools. The doctor went through various instructions and cautions to take surrounding the stoma, and I remember João being adamant that he did not want that to happen.

I felt for my husband so much. Imagine having your whole life change in front of your eyes, not being able to perform bodily functions the way you've been programmed to do them for your whole life. However, the most important thing to us was his health. If that meant a stoma, the whole family would listen intently to the instructions so we could help him through it.

The day of the procedure drew near. Fear dominated us. João provided us with his account numbers out of concern that he would not make it through the procedure alive. Things felt real the moment João gave us access to his banking accounts out of fear he would not make it through the procedure. He had always been protective, and even in hardship, he only thought about how his family would survive. He was always prepared for the worst.

With both of us unemployed, we didn't have much saved, so we frantically applied for grants, funds, and any sort of help out there. Macmillian provided us with financial support. Although it didn't cover our bills or expenses, it was an extremely helpful amount, and we were immensely grateful for it in our time of need.

On the day of the operation, João had to be in by seven in the morning, so Catarina and I drove him to the hospital whilst my three other children were at school. I remember asking him if I could inform our families of what was happening, but João said we could talk about it later. We sat with him for less than ten minutes before he was called in. The nurse instructed us to go home, and I just thought to myself, *My God, they must be in a hurry!* We didn't have a chance to give him a big hug to comfort him, but we always prayed for his recovery. From the day João was diagnosed until that day, he had suffered a lot of pain. When he called me at 9 a.m.

to tell me he was still sitting in the waiting room, all I could do was cry because I knew it was hurting him, and I wasn't sitting next to him. I had been fasting and praying for my husband in the days leading up to his operation, so when I got home, I continued. I did everything I could, but still felt guilty for not being at his side.

João was already undergoing surgery when I arrived at the hospital, so I waited a while in the waiting room before going to the chapel to pray. That day, I had placed what felt like over fifty calls to João, starting from 9.30 a.m. until 3 p.m., asking him how he felt and if the doctors had seen him yet, but I could tell that all I was doing was stressing him more. I placed another fifty calls to the hospital to ask if the operation had gone well and if I could see my husband but was always met by the same response: 'We will call you when we have any news.'

When a doctor called out my name, it was about 11 o'clock at night. I ran towards him in anticipation, holding my breath until he said, 'Helena, the surgery is finished. Everything went according to plan, and a stoma was not required.'

I just broke down into tears and asked him, 'Are you the doctor who operated on my husband?'

When he replied, 'Yes,' I sobbed and thanked him profusely. I lost count of how many times.

I asked if I could see him, to which the doctor replied, 'Yes. Later, someone will come to get you, so you can go and see him.'

The happiness I felt at that moment was immeasurable. When I told my daughters the good news—that Daddy didn't need to have a stoma and the procedure went smoothly—I was yelling. It was met with even more yelling from them. 'Glory to God. Glory to God!' were the only words we managed to get out.

Catarina insisted that she and Jessica were on the way to the hospital to see their dad, but I told them to wait until the next day. Catarina is stubborn and a daddy's girl, so, in her true nature, she was outside of the hospital with Jessica in twenty minutes flat.

Anticipation built as we waited. It worsened when I walked in to see him lying there, connected to a multitude of tubes and machines.

The moment he saw me, his smile widened, and he giggled. 'My wife,' and a few tears escaped. They weren't tears of sadness, but of joy and relief. He was very happy when I told him he didn't need to use a stoma, and he asked me how I knew. When I told him that the doctor had informed me, he became even more joyful.

I told him the girls were coming to visit him, and he said, 'Helena, it is late.' Tell them to come tomorrow.' He knew his daughter, Catarina, was stubborn, so he also knew there was no way they would return home.

João's recovery room didn't allow for many visitors to prevent contamination, and my daughters called me upset, saying they were not allowed in by the nurses, and I could hear the frustration in their voices. I remember pleading with the nurses, who said they could go in quickly, but that I couldn't be inside, too, so I ran outside to let them know.

When I saw them sitting there, waiting patiently, it was an indescribable moment, a joy to see my girls, hope, my life with João, and the love we share for one another. The girls ran in to embrace their father, comforting him, and giggling away with him. While I waited, I called my friend to share the wonderful news with her, and of course, we both fell victim to inconsolable tears of excitement.

At around 1 a.m., the girls said, 'We love you, *Papai*! We will be here tomorrow,' and I went in to say the same since I wasn't permitted to stay overnight.

CHAPTER 5

TELLING MY FAMILY

The following morning, I had to get up early to drop the kids off at school. As Camilla and João Carlos and I were eating breakfast, I spoke to them about their father. I informed them that he was in the hospital after having belly surgery, but everything was fine with him. I also told them that when they finished school, we would all be visiting their father there. They were both happy and sad because they wanted to be there for him, but we'd always kept Daddy's sickness a secret from them. First of all, they were simply too young to understand, and they had no knowledge of the condition or what cancer was. To put that burden on them when they were that young felt malicious, so instead, we decided to tell them their father had a gut ache and needed surgery to get better.

João was in the same room when I arrived at the hospital. I was concerned because they had told me he would be there for a few hours in case something went wrong. However, the moment I saw him, all I could do was smile; my husband was so gorgeous.

I was so relieved to see him and his beautiful blue eyes beaming at me, but I had to ask the nurse if everything was all right with him. She replied that he was in that room while they waited for a bed to move him to another level. Knowing that he was stable, and the procedure had gone well, I knew it was time to inform the family of both the operation and the cancer.

João agreed, but he pleaded with me not to tell his family for the simple fact that they were elderly and facing their own health issues, and he didn't want them to worry about him. I respected his wishes, of course, stepped out into the hallway, and recorded a video explaining everything. I sent it to my family's group chat on WhatsApp.

In minutes, I was flooded with calls, texts, and a million questions, even though I'd asked them not to worry. Everyone, including me, began crying. My family was very understanding of the news, and when I asked that no one tell my mother the situation due to her own health issues, they all complied.

I went to pay attention to João because it was finally time for him to move to another room. The girls went to pick up the kids from school, and they came straight to the hospital to see their father. João was overjoyed to see the little ones and have his entire family present with him. It was difficult for me to leave the hospital and my husband there because I already missed him when I was at home. I was afraid to leave him there and sleep alone, so I kept the lights on when I was at home.

The following day, I had to tend to some business, so I went to the hospital later. At the bus stop, my husband called me in pain and said that he believed the operation had not gone well because the stitches they had placed in his intestine had opened. As he described the agony he was experiencing, I felt horrible and had to ask if he had spoken to a doctor. He told me that he had not yet, only the nurse. I urged him to tell the doctor so he could help him. I tried to reassure him that the stitches hadn't opened, and maybe the pain he felt was because he had recently eaten, and as the food moved through his intestines, it caused pressure on the stitches. I wasn't fully convinced, but I had to search for some positivity.

After calming him down, I went to my meeting with a heavy heart, but I could barely sit still, so I excused myself, telling everyone I wasn't feeling too well and needed time off.

I went straight to the hospital to look after him. He was still in immense pain, but I needed to care for him. I took him to the bathroom, gave him a bath, and tried to calm him down.

When the doctors arrived, I felt a little hopeful as he told us the stitches hadn't opened, or his stomach would be swollen. He said that my reason was correct: his pain was due to his body getting used to everything post-procedure.

João had been in the hospital for three days at that point. Prior to his procedure, he was due to take a test to become an Uber driver, which he had already paid £200 for. On Friday, I advised João not to cancel since I was confident he would be discharged in time to complete the exam; otherwise, he would have to wait another whole month and lose out on that £200. The test was then booked for the following Wednesday.

Sunday came around. I attended church with my children, and my uncle joined us. I eventually told him the news, and I could see his heart break. He and João had known each other for decades, and my uncle loved João a lot, so I knew it was hard for him to accept. Luckily, our church was right next to the hospital, so we were never too far from my husband.

That day, I brought a bottle of water with me to church so the priest could bless it and I could give it to my husband. I remember walking up to the priest, asking him to bless the water, and telling him about my husband, who was in the hospital post-operation to remove the cancer. He simply asked which hospital he was at.

When I replied, 'Royal London Hospital,' he responded with, 'I will come with you to the hospital so I can personally pray for him.' At that moment, the adrenaline, happiness, and faith that ignited within me felt incredible. I just looked at the priest and thanked him. I never expected him to go out of his way to follow us to the hospital, but I was grateful for his hope and faith, and it fuelled my strength.

God is the greatest!

When we arrived at the hospital, all of the nurses stopped and stared in confusion as there were nine of us altogether, wanting to see my husband. I quickly explained that we were all family and just wanted to pray for him. Thankfully, they let us in. I can laugh at this today, but as soon as João saw all of us, he was terrified. I can only imagine the thoughts going through his head at that moment, thinking his life was over. I reassured him that the priest was just there to pray, and that's exactly what we did. We all stood and prayed for my husband to feel better, to have a speedy recovery, and for the cancer to completely leave his body.

We all believed in the power of healing, including my husband, because with God, everything was possible.

CHAPTER 6

GREAT EXPECTATION

On Monday, he was finally released from the hospital after a whole week away from his family. We were ecstatic and jumping with joy, but he was still very weak. Our prayers never stopped.

Wednesday came around. He couldn't walk properly and was still really weak, but he wanted to take the test. I had faith that everything would turn out okay.

After travelling for one hour and thirty minutes, he went upstairs to take the test as I waited for him. It was over after about an hour.

João came down, feeling weak and lightheaded, and I regretted letting him take the test whilst in recovery. He fell asleep as soon as we arrived at our house.

A week later and the results came in: João had received a perfect score on the test to become an Uber driver, and we were ecstatic. I remember all of my children chanting and João's big smile. We were so proud of him for doing so well. Even in the condition he was in, he was our hero. It taught us all an important lesson: when we really want something; we do everything in our power to make it happen. Even battling cancer, we received many victories along the way.

God is wonderful.

With João in recovery and me out of work, I felt as if I needed something to do so I could make some money since I was at home, taking care of the family. I told a friend I was considering making dolls again so I could start selling them—that was my job in Portugal before we left—but I didn't have my industrial sewing machine anymore. She turned to me and suggested that I buy a used sewing machine, and she opened her eBay and started looking.

We were sitting in the park, bidding on auctions, when I found one, bid on it, and won the auction. I was overjoyed with the new sewing machine I managed to buy for £100. We had to collect the machine from the seller's house, and it was quite far, but at that point, João was feeling better and of course, wanted to make his wife as happy as always, so we both went to get the machine.

The couple who sold it to us were an interracial couple like us, and I couldn't help but smile at the coincidence. The machine did need some adjustments, but my husband has always been a handyman, so he got to work straight away. João has always been like that, a hard worker, strong, and resilient, and I knew it made him happy to feel as if he could still help out his family despite the illness.

I produced dolls in two months and was actively looking for venues to sell them. I first sold my dolls at the children's school. Then, I found a fun fair that would let me set up a stall, and I could sell all my creations for three days for a small fee. The fair was huge, and I knew it was a great opportunity, so I stayed up until two in the morning, working, so I had enough stock to generate sales. It was something I really enjoyed because it allowed me to take care of my family and take my husband to his hospital appointments, but I didn't have the financial stability our family needed. I kept looking for part-time employment so I would have time for school runs and taking care of João, as well as working on my dolls; I was basically searching for a miracle.

After applying for a number of jobs and attending multiple interviews, I finally came across one that was ideal. It was supposed to be a cashier's position, where I had to arrive at 10 a.m. and leave at 2 p.m. They promised to contact me after the interview, and I waited, but by the time a month had passed, I had already given up hope.

We were excited yet concerned when we learned that João would need another surgery on 8 July. I always accompanied him when he had chemotherapy so I could provide him with some form of support. While I waited for the chemo to end, I sat by his side, making dolls. Every time João had chemotherapy, he returned home with a bottle that delivered more chemotherapy to the rest of his body through a tube in a vein. The nurses had to come over to our house to detach the bottle and tube, and every time they did, he was unwell for five days; he recovered and felt good for a week. Then he would have chemotherapy again and feel sick again. It felt like a constant cycle of good and bad, but thank God, it was, at least, helping him.

I was making dolls to go to this fantastic fair when I realised I hadn't heard back about that job, and I told myself it was time to start looking for new jobs. With one week left to go before João's surgery, I was sitting at home when I got a call from the dream job I really wanted. They talked me through the role and invited me to come in the next day for a final interview.

The next day, I arrived at Canary Wharf, outside all of the big buildings. After seeing the work and immediately liking it, I accepted the position, and I couldn't believe it. Since I would be working at a global bank, they had to fulfil different types of checks that would take approximately two to three weeks. I was thrilled since I would have time to care for my family, and the work was close to my house.

The day for João's liver surgery to remove the cancer arrived. This time, I remained in the hospital until the procedure was over. While I was waiting, I got a call from my new work, telling me I could start the following day. I couldn't believe what I was hearing. The position was everything I could have asked for, and with my doll business as well, it would be a big help at home with the bills.

I accepted to start the job the following day, even though my husband was currently having surgery, and I was unsure of how it was going. I trusted my emotions and faith in my decision.

I began praying to God after hanging up the phone, pleading with him that everything would go well with the operation.

The wonderful news arrived. The doctor came over to reassure me that everything went extremely well, and I could go in to see my husband. They also informed me they had removed all of the tumours they discovered during the scan. 'How many tumours?' I questioned.

Just when I was glad they had taken everything from him, the doctor said that one tumour was concealed behind the other, so it hadn't appeared on the scan.

When I went to meet João, he was completely different this time, in more agony, and more perplexed. He was pleased when I told him about the position, and he liked that it was close to both our home and the hospital, so I could pick up the kids and take them to school.

The following day, I was scheduled to begin work, and I thoroughly enjoyed my first day there. When I finished, I hurried to the hospital to visit João, who was still in agony but nonetheless delighted to see me, despite the fact he had been there for more than a week. He was getting tired of hospitals at that point, and I could see it in him.

My sister was getting married in Portugal in August, and João and I were asked to be the godparents. Because of João's surgery, we wanted to decline the invitation, but my sister insisted that if we declined, the wedding would not be the same. Despite our hesitation, we booked the boat and drove to Portugal. Although João wasn't one hundred per cent, he planned to drive, but he didn't drive much because it had only been almost a month since the operation, and he was still in pain; Catarina would drive most of the trip to take the burden from João.

When we first arrived in Portugal, we went straight to my in-laws' house. João's family was unaware of what was going on with him, and when my mother-in-law hugged him, she started to cry and said, 'My son, you are not well. You are sick.'

João's brother also thought it odd that he was so thin. When we got inside the house, my mother-in-law asked me what was wrong with João, and I told her to ask her son. She sobbed and turned to João, who she questioned. He proceeded to lie once more about what was wrong.

I overheard and informed my mother-in-law that her son had cancer and had undergone surgery. As I was tired of concealing the truth, I said, 'I don't think it's fair for my family to know everything when his own family doesn't.'

João gave me a furious look because he didn't want them to know anything. My father-in-law also began to cry, and he questioned me about whether it was malignant cancer. João quickly responded, 'No,' but they already knew the answer.

I looked at João and immediately stopped talking about the subject.

The following day, João's brother once more asked me to tell him the truth, so I did. I told him that João had cancer, that he had already undergone two operations to remove it, and that he would begin treatment again with chemotherapy once he returned to London. He said he already suspected that was the case. At that point, the only people who knew everything about João were his brother and his uncle from Lisbon.

We spent four days in the north of Portugal before going to Lisbon to see my family. Although my family already knew about his condition, when we arrived in Portugal, João's face seemed to improve significantly, and he no longer appeared to be sick. Everyone was pleased to see him in that condition.

João greatly assisted my sister with the wedding preparations, and he never stopped helping the entire time we were in Lisbon.

The wedding went very well, and we had a few days off to unwind a little from everything, so we travelled to Albufeira, Portugal, and made some really beautiful memories there.

CHAPTER 7

BRING THE PAIN

We returned back to the UK, and I went back to work. João was scheduled to begin chemo again on 8 September. When he began chemo, the cycle commenced again: the days of vomiting; the week spent feeling terrible, and the next feeling a little better. I was still making my dolls and working. I was not generating as much money as I would have liked, but it was enough to handle all of the household expenses.

I dropped the kids off at school and then had to tend to my husband, my home, and my business when I got home. I was so exhausted. I was still going to the handcraft and DIY fairs on the weekend when I realised João had developed numerous pimples all over his body and a fever that wouldn't go away for two weeks.

This was around November, and with João's birthday slowly approaching, I wanted to make it as special as possible for him and throw him a surprise party. I hired someone to make his cake and prepare all the snacks. I spent a significant amount of money buying the decorations for the party, but when João's fever persisted, I knew we had to go back to the hospital.

After waiting five hours, I couldn't believe what I heard: the doctors ordered him to stay in the hospital so they could monitor him and perform checks. He had a fever that wouldn't go away for a whole month and was coughing up a lot of phlegm, but doctors were still unable to determine what was wrong and how they could help. I immediately took time off work to care for him, the kids, and myself.

João was placed in a special room reserved for patients with contagious diseases because of the fever, and I was the only one allowed to visit him; the children weren't allowed. The tests they performed on him yielded no findings.

There were three days until his birthday, and he was still in the hospital. I cancelled the party with all the guests, but I was unable to cancel the things I had already paid for. The kids wanted to see him, but he would need to be moved to another room for that to happen, and the doctors wouldn't authorise it.

João's birthday came, and we sang Happy Birthday to him over a video call with me, our children, and my friend, while he was in bed in the hospital. The moment was both beautiful and sad.

The following day, I went to the hospital and brought him a piece of cake. I also prepared healthy meals and green juices for him throughout his nineteen-day stay in the hospital.

His cough and fever continued throughout the month, and doctors were puzzled as to what it might be. Looking back on it now, I believe he had COVID-19 at the time, but it was November 2019, and no one knew of the existence of coronavirus back then.

His fever went down, and the doctors released him. We finally had our hero back at home with us, and it felt as if everything went back to normal while he was recovering, and I went back to work.

Nothing was the same at work. My manager treated me poorly. I think it was masked annoyance at the fact I had missed ten days of work to care for my husband, but I did not regret it at all. In fact, I would have happily lost my job to take care of my husband. I would do it again and again, in this lifetime and the next.

My dream career had turned into a nightmare, and I only went to work because I had to. I continued to participate in various craft fairs and even made a website so I could sell my dolls online, which generated enough money to help with expenses.

We were relieved when João resumed chemotherapy after it had been temporarily halted due to his fever. Well, we were happy that something was being done to aid his illness.

In the meantime, I did not enjoy work anymore. My manager talked behind my back about how unprofessional it was of me to start a new job and take so many days off, which I understood, but he had no idea of the suffering my family was enduring behind closed doors.

After hearing what he said, I went to talk to him and explained the situation to him so that no one at work would be aware of what was happening to my family and me. He pledged not to tell anyone, and our relationship improved significantly until everyone at work began treating me differently. He, in fact, told everyone that my husband had cancer and that I believed I should be afforded more privileges in the company. I never had and never would say anything like that because it was our secret, something I didn't want to share with the world. I had never had a boss like that, one who gossiped more than he worked. I absolutely detested him, so I quit work. I told myself that, with God's help, I wouldn't need to work for anyone else.

I was still selling my dolls, and João was still receiving treatment; however, when news of coronavirus broke, João's treatments stopped, my dolls were no longer in demand, and we were unable to leave the house.

As someone who was at high risk, João stayed at home for three months without leaving the house for anything. Jessica had moved back home from Birmingham, where she was studying for university, and Catarina started working from home, so we were all together at home again, finally.

With nothing to keep us occupied, Camilla started making videos on an app called TikTok. I had seen her make a few with Catarina and then with her brother, João Carlos, and was entertained by the idea of it. Catarina eventually started making TikTok videos, too, and she invited her dad and me to do one in which she would dunk our heads into a bowl of water after a question. We were so confused by the idea, but she posted it, and it ended up gaining a lot of views and comments. By the second video with us, people started enquiring as to whether my husband and I had our own TikTok account, so I said, why not?

CHAPTER 8

CREATOR

I first created our TikTok account with the name 'Vilarcouple' although João didn't want to make as many videos with me, despite my constant begging. He didn't feel comfortable making videos with the PICC line in his arm as he didn't want everyone to know, so I began making videos alone and with my children. I always knew it was meant to be my husband's and my page, so I begged him one more time. I even cried a little, and we eventually made our first video, dancing to 'Jerusalema' by Master KG.

The video got a lot of views, and we were happy, so we made another dance video and that got a lot of views, too. That was when I knew that was what I should be doing until João decided he didn't want to do it anymore.

I changed the username to 'justhelena43' and decided to make videos by myself since he didn't want to. It wasn't long before I asked him to make videos with me again. I was surrounded by couples making videos together on TikTok, and I wanted him with me. I told him how much I loved him and that he loved me, too, so we should do it together, but he wasn't changing his mind.

João left the house for the first time in three months to go to an appointment. After the appointment, we went to the supermarket to do some shopping, and João stayed in the car and waited for me. When I got in the car, I told him that I was making a quick video for TikTok, that I'd only show a little bit of him, and he didn't have to do anything. He wasn't happy about it, but he accepted, and we made the video.

The video went viral on TikTok. We started gaining a lot of followers, and people wanted to see more. I started making more videos for TikTok, and it did us a lot of good. João felt like himself again, smiling and laughing with pleasure, and I did, too. This newfound love for creating content kept me happy. It let me be creative and come up with ideas for new videos. It allowed me to think outside the box and to take writing this book more seriously. I want you to understand how these videos have not only helped bring a smile to your faces but to ours, too. I want you to understand how grateful we are for all of your love and support because those videos allowed me to create new dreams and reach heights I never expected. Because of all my followers, I have the courage to come forward publicly to share our story and the hardships we faced. Because of you, I am fulfilling a lifelong dream of mine to write this, even if it is through our most terrible nightmare. That's the only appropriate word, a nightmare because to me, it still feels as if I am sleeping, and that one day, I will wake up and realise it was all a dream, that everything I have endured as a mother and as a wife was a lie, as was everything I've lived as a mother and woman.

A lot of people see the love I feel for my husband when I look at him in our videos. This love of ours is beautiful, and every day it gets stronger. When I look at my husband and see how strong he is, I get a new sense of respect and pride in him. He has been through so much and will always try to put his best foot forward and be full of life wherever he goes.

Eventually, I did a lot of videos alone because João was not always well due to his starting chemo again. When he felt well, he would join in, but that wasn't often because he didn't feel comfortable making videos due to the chemo bottle and PICC line in his arm.

When João started the treatment again, he began vomiting; he was weak; he did not sleep at night, and we noticed that he was losing hair on his head and in his eyebrows. When he was well again, we recorded a lot of videos. More and more people wanted to see us, and we grew on TikTok. I had my private Instagram with the same name, 'justhelena43'. I never accepted anyone's requests to follow me on that page because it was private, and only my family and friends were there, but I accepted a request from an account called 'BWWM'. I had never heard of that page in my life, but their profile was full of photos of couples, specifically interracial couples. I found the concept of the page beautiful, and I accepted their request.

One day, I was in bed with João and my Instagram was blowing up with notifications. I had no idea what was going on, but as soon as I went on the app, I saw 300 follow requests, and I was shocked. On this private account, I only had 105 followers, and I was fine with that number. I did not understand why so many people suddenly wanted to follow me until I saw that the BWWM account had followed me days before, posted a video of João and me, and tagged us.

I couldn't believe it, but I was so excited by this new venture that I spoke to João, and said it was time for me to take my account off of its private status to make it public. When I woke up, I was at six hundred followers. Another three days went by, and I was at 1,500 followers. The numbers just kept growing on Instagram and TikTok because the videos João and I made together on TikTok went viral and reached thousands of people who seemed to really like the idea of our marriage because they kept following and sharing our videos.

I created a video with João where the concept was him telling me he was going out and that I shouldn't bother him, but whilst he was talking, his hands were shaking to show he was scared of me. I remember doing the same video three times so it could be the way we wanted, and the comedic aspect wasn't lost. I captioned it 'When your wife is African!' The caption was simply to grab people's attention, and that's exactly what it did. In less than twenty-four hours, we reached one million views after that video and gained 20,000 followers on our account. I could not believe it. We were overjoyed with it.

I remember João laughing so much over the video. Every time he opened our TikTok, he laughed at himself and the way he was shaking in the video. I realised that he was happier now, making these videos. He smiled and laughed more. It seemed as if his whole mood had changed despite feeling sick with the chemo.

I researched videos, and we made a lot of them in our own style. We found a lot of TikTok trends, but we were more interested in creating content we liked. At the time, there were a lot of dances going viral, but we didn't know how to dance and found them really complicated, so we danced our own way and had so much fun along the way. Our 'VilarFamily' grew everywhere, across all of our social media, and we couldn't believe the success.

We started receiving direct messages, and we had a few people asking why we were not on YouTube; we just hadn't given it any thought until then.

We started our YouTube channel, which was a very different avenue for us. Everyone does not like YouTube, nor do they have YouTube, so the numbers of followers on YouTube were always very different, and they did not grow as much.

I wanted to make more and more videos so we could keep growing, but João was still doing chemo, and it seemed the new treatment was causing a lot of pimples on his body and his face. We did make a few videos whilst he was like that, but we eventually stopped because I didn't want to press him. I saw that he was getting very weak, and the pimples were affecting his confidence. All I wanted was for him to be happy.

I decided to continue making videos, even if I had to do them alone, because at that point, TikTok started to pay us a little, and the more videos we made, the more money we could make. Due to COVID-19, I began making masks and bows along with my dolls. With the new income from social media, I felt a little more relaxed and not as stressed about the finances.

João went for a checkup, and they saw the colon cancer had returned, but it was not big, so the doctors decided that this time, they would give him radiotherapy where the tumour was. Thankfully, the tumour was only in his colon and had not spread to the rest of his body.

He began doing radiotherapy every day for five weeks, and it seemed to be going well as he could go to the hospital and return home alone, as he did not feel unwell after it.

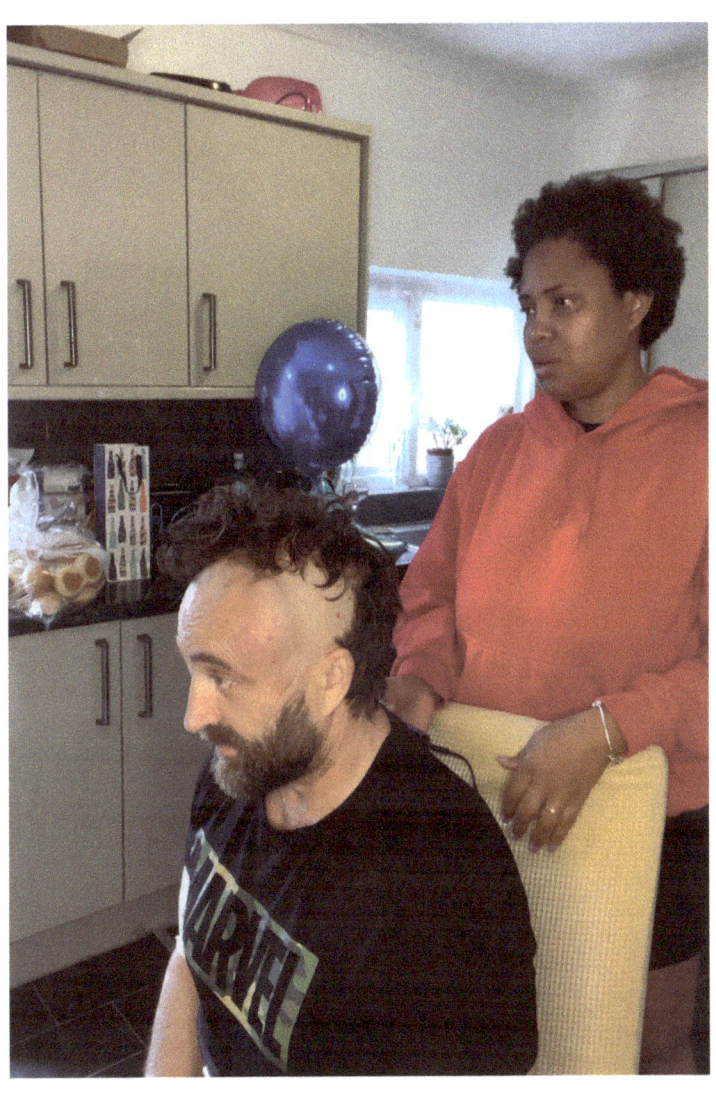

CHAPTER 9

TORN INTO PIECES

João showed me something he had on his forehead, something that had never been there before.

I told him to stop looking for things that were not there.

It was something very small, around the size of a grain of rice. After two weeks of radiotherapy, what had looked like a grain of rice had manifested itself to the size of a bean, or even a little bigger. That was where the doctors failed my husband.

João was still concerned, so he showed the doctor, who told him, 'It is impossible for cancer to grow there.' João was adamant, so the doctor ordered a biopsy, taking a tissue sample from his forehead just to be sure. With one week left of radiotherapy, the whole family was happy that João would finally be cancer free.

Because Jessica lived in Birmingham at the time for university, I called to give her updates, and she cried when I told her there was only one week left and things were looking good for João.

He was still being monitored and having checkups to monitor the cancer in his colon.

I told João that we were going to start making a lot of videos now since there was nothing to stop us now that he was better. When I insisted we make more videos, it was not for fame, but for us to make money. When we created viral videos, the money helped us with bills and daily living.

The week went by, and the radiotherapy was finally over. João returned from that last radiotherapy session looking gloomy and told me he had some bad news. My heart sank, but I tried not to worry and just asked him what was going on. What he said next changed our lives forever.

He started by saying the results from the biopsy had returned, and the doctor told him the mass growing on his forehead was, indeed, cancer.

I couldn't believe it. I could not understand why this was happening to my João. My world collapsed for what felt like the millionth time, and it hurt worse because this time, my husband had to give me that news, and I didn't know how to comfort him. I felt hurt and angry towards the doctors who hadn't believed him sooner. All I could do at that moment was hug my husband and soak his clothes with my tears.

My daughter, Catarina, who was working from home, had heard the commotion and came to us. She was worried and kept asking what was going on, so I told her. I could see the devastation on her face, and within seconds, she was crying as she couldn't believe what was happening either.

We knew we had to tell Jessica, too, but we also knew the approach had to be different. Jessica has always been the more sensitive daughter, and with her being three hours away at university, we didn't want to worry her too much. She loved her dad so much, but I knew that bad news would trigger her, and her mental health would suffer. The last thing we had told her was that there was no cancer present, so when we called to let her know it was back, I heard her heart break over the phone as she cried.

It broke my heart to see my children suffer like that. We had many plans together, and it felt as if they were all lost again. The suffering and pain had once again returned.

João had an appointment with the doctor where they would tell him more about the size and best treatment option. I went with João to the consultation, and when we got there, there was another doctor there from Ecology, along with three students in the room. João and I sat down, ready to receive more bad news.

The doctor started by showing the MRI João had done and said the cancer in his head was growing aggressively and getting bigger day by day. He said it had almost reached the brain.

Oh my God!

Once again, I could not believe what I was hearing. First, the doctor had told him it was impossible for it to be cancer. They hadn't believed him for so long, and now the cancer was growing aggressively to the point where it had almost reached his brain.

I looked at João, and as always, he was super calm, and as always, I started to cry.

The doctor said the best option would be to operate as soon as possible. She explained to me how they would proceed, that they would remove the tumour and a part of the bone in the forehead and then put a graft on the head. It sounded terrifying, and it only got worse when she began talking about possible risks and complications. This was when the tension in the room grew, and it felt as if João and I had stopped breathing. Internal bleeding, loss of speech, loss of movement—each risk hit us like a tonne of bricks. It felt as if we were in a movie, being told the worst possible news whilst everything else around us blurred and disappeared whilst we wallowed in sadness.

We left the consultation feeling shattered.

As soon as we got home, we talked to our oldest daughters about what had happened, and João informed us all that he did not want to have the operation because of the possible risks. I knew he would rather have radiotherapy first and then chemo to try to reduce the tumour, and to him, the operation should be the last resort.

The girls and I didn't agree with that idea at first because the doctor had said the surgery was the best option, but my husband and his wishes always came first. It was already a devastating position to be in, and we wanted him to feel as comfortable as possible and make whatever decision felt right for him.

We respected his decision, and João went on to call the doctor to let them know of his decision. She reassured him it was not the best option because the cancer was growing fast and aggressively, and radiotherapy was out of the question. They eventually managed to convince João to go through with the surgery, and it was scheduled for the following week. It felt like a relief when we were all on the same page and happy to proceed.

João had another appointment during that week so he could do all of his checkups and tests to ensure he was prepared for the surgery.

Monday morning came around, and we were on our way to do some shopping at Costco to ensure we had all the essentials for his operation the following day.

What happened next was challenging for us to understand, but now, as a family, we collectively feel as though the doctors and everyone in charge of my husband's health failed him, essentially robbing him of a long and healthy life.

On the drive there, João received a call from the doctor, telling him the surgery that was supposed to take place the next day had been cancelled because other tests he had done showed the cancer in his liver and lungs had returned, and the best option now was for him to have radiotherapy and then chemotherapy. It was just a never-ending cycle of bad news. João was always calm whilst I panicked and didn't know how to process the news.

After convincing João, who is a very stubborn man, to have the surgery, getting him prepared both physically and mentally, and then just cancelling on him felt wrong and unfair. The cancer in his body was still growing day by day.

CHAPTER 10

FALSE HOPE

*W*hen I got out of the car to go shopping, I felt as if I could no longer walk. I felt all the strength leave my body until João took my hand and guided me inside. The one suffering through the physical pain was also the one comforting me. He was the only reason I was strong.

We didn't speak about the phone call whilst shopping. When we got home, we knew we had to talk to the girls again about the new development, and it always felt like the hardest thing in the world delivering the news to them, especially Jessica—how could we comfort a child who was so far away from us? It felt like a dark cloud of sadness had re-entered our home after that day.

As a firm believer in God, I told my family that it was time to strengthen our connection to God because with Him, all things were possible, and it was only by His grace that we had been able to endure all of our hardships.

We all started to pray more. We would kneel in the living room or in my and João's bedroom, holding each other's hands and praying for the cancer to leave João's body. Ever since the doctor had given João the news, his mood changed. He was depressed and didn't want to talk to anyone, let alone leave his bedroom. I think that was the moment it officially hit João.

The tumour on his forehead had not stopped growing. It doubled in size and made his face very swollen.

The weekend had come around; I remember it vividly. João got out of bed that Saturday morning, took a look at himself in the mirror, was not happy with his appearance, and went straight back to bed. When I brought him breakfast that morning, I could not believe what I saw. My husband is so handsome—to me, he will always be the most handsome man on Earth—but that moment, when I looked at him, I did not recognise him.

His face was swollen to the point where he couldn't even open his eyes. I was genuinely shocked. João and I were always the best of friends; we always talked about everything, sharing every little secret and thought, but ever since he got the news, he did not talk to me anymore. I just wanted to be able to help him, but I did not know how.

My daughter called the nurse to let them know that his face was swollen and told them there was no way he could wait another two weeks to start treatment because the tumour was already too big.

The nurse agreed and scheduled the appointment for five days' time. She also said that João had to start taking steroids to relieve the swelling.

João struggled to take the medication. There were times when he would lie and say he had taken the steroids when he hadn't. I never quite understood why he did this, but I believe they made him feel unwell or not quite like himself. I will never know, because at the time, João didn't talk to me as much about any pain he was having.

I asked him if I could make a video on social media to explain that João would no longer be making videos, but he refused, along with Jessica, who felt it was best to keep this a private matter. My daughter, Catarina, was, however, okay with my making the video, so I was very conflicted.

The next day, I went back to talk to João, and before I had even finished my sentence, he said, 'Yes, you can do the video,' and I felt relieved. I made a video for our YouTube channel, explaining everything we had gone through from the beginning up until that point. I had never published a video on our YouTube channel that got so many views in such a short time. The video I published was simple, it was not edited well or anything, but it was just the raw video. I couldn't do anything with the video because anytime I tried, I just shed tears.

I released the video as is and named it 'We have a secret'. I also posted a short video to all of our social media explaining that João would not be able to make any more videos for now and that we had a YouTube video explaining why.

In seconds, we were flooded with so much support, love, and affection. We received thousands of prayers from across the world, which I would never have expected in a million years, but it felt so good to know we had everyone's support. It felt like such a relief to know that we didn't have to hide the truth anymore, to know that we did not have to live in silence. God was in control of everything.

Despite the support, I knew João was still really down, as he spent most of his time in our room. The weather was nice that day, and I called him down to catch some rays and sunbathe. We sat together in the garden, but it felt different. He wouldn't really look at me, and I felt like crying inside.

I filmed little videos next to him to try to entertain him to see if I could get back the husband I knew.

The man sitting beside me was not my husband. He was sad and wouldn't smile that same beautiful smile as much anymore. João was no longer João.

CHAPTER 11

BROKEN

A week later, we headed to the first radiotherapy consultation, where they wanted to make an impression of his head so they would have a mould of the growing mass. I found it super interesting how they made the mould, as I had never seen it done before and didn't know it was even a possibility.

The next day, João was to have his first radiotherapy session on the mass on his forehead, and everything went very well. The second session also went smoothly. By the time he received the third radiotherapy session on a Friday, he was feeling okay, so the whole family sat there in the living room, watching a movie together, which was one of our favourite activities to do as a family. Jessica was coming down to London more often now—sometimes on a weekly basis—so having her there made it feel like everything had gone back to normal, and there were no worries in the world.

Saturday came around, and I went shopping. I bought a lot of vegetables to make João some healthier food options.

I prepared soup for him while he was lying in bed, along with some carrot juice, as it is said to help fight cancer. However, when I went upstairs, I saw that he was vomiting everything back up. He had been able to eat on Friday, but by Saturday, his body was rejecting everything. He drank water and vomited. He ate and vomited. At that point, I became really worried and didn't know how to best help him, but I decided it was best if he rested a little.

Some hours went by, and João was still resting, so I called the ambulance.

By the time the paramedics arrived, João was up, and they gave him medication to help ease his nausea. We asked if it was necessary for him to go to the hospital, and they said no, that it was unnecessary for him to wait five hours to be seen, only for the doctors to tell him the same thing they had. They explained it away as being a side effect of the radiotherapy. They said again that if the vomiting had not stopped, he would have had to go to hospital.

It was around 4 o'clock in the morning when João started vomiting again, and I told him I would call the ambulance. João, being stubborn, told me no, but when he said it, he began vomiting again, so I picked up the phone and called the ambulance.

When they arrived, they wanted to take him to the hospital, and I wanted to go with him, but they would not let me because of COVID regulations. João was a bit confused by then, saying random things that didn't make much sense. I knew he wasn't feeling like himself when he said he wanted to go to the hospital alone, and I began to worry.

The ambulance took him straight to the hospital so he could be seen by his doctor, and I stayed with the children, waiting for someone to call me. I called João, but he wasn't able to talk to me, so I just started panicking and wishing I could be with my husband.

About four hours later, the doctor had some test results, and he called me to ask how long my husband had been confused, telling me that he wasn't making much sense. I said it had been a few days, but it was just little errors, like accidentally calling Jessica by Catarina's name, so we didn't think too much of it. It wasn't until the weekend that we noticed and made sense of it, as it had got progressively worse.

My daughter drove to pick him up from the hospital, and he was prescribed more tablets. He came home and was no longer throwing up, so I made him some rice soup, which he ate along with a sandwich, and we were happy he managed to keep it down.

Monday came, and he had another radiotherapy session. He began struggling to walk and said that his vision was blurry, so I called an Uber, and we went to the hospital. He did his treatment, but I noticed that he was getting progressively worse. He had no strength in his legs, his face was looking a little pale, and he looked like a zombie. He still wasn't making much sense, but the next day, he went in to have his last session.

During the last treatment, the nurse came over to ask me if everything was okay with João, and I informed her that I had noticed he had been confused in the last couple of days. He was forgetting things easily, becoming weak, and had vomited the past weekend, and I saw her face drop. She looked very worried and said she would talk to the doctor who would come and talk to me.

When we saw the doctor, I explained everything to her again, and she started asking João maths questions. Anyone who knows João knows how good he is at maths, so when she asked him a simple question he could not answer, she got worried and told us we had to go upstairs to do some tests.

When we got there, we saw the nurses making a bed. I thought it was strange and asked if it was for my husband, and she said, 'Yes.'

João stayed at the hospital, and I went home to tell our children the news. The older ones were rather relieved because in the hospital, he really had to take the medication.

When I went to see him the next day, I spoke to the nurse before I went to see him and asked her how he was doing. She told me that he had slept well, he was fine, and then she told me that I should try to convince João to put on his pyjamas because they had already tried, and he did not want to put them on.

I went to João with the pyjamas in my hand to convince him to put them on, and I found him lying in the hospital bed with his jeans and t-shirt on and his hat on his head. I couldn't see his face because he was wearing a mask, and I just thought to myself that he was just being stubborn, but I knew that he didn't get changed into the pyjamas because he detested hospitals and didn't want to stay any longer. It was like a statement he had to make.

I walked in, put the bags on the floor and began taking off his jeans so I could change him into something more comfortable. My husband, who I have been with for over 25 years, did not want me to change him. He did not want me to take off his boxers or be naked next to me. I think a part of him felt embarrassed because he was so weak and couldn't do it himself. I cry when I look back on this and think of how much he had to have been hurting physically and mentally.

I took him to the bathroom and sat and chatted with him whilst he took a bath. I got him changed and lying in bed, and hours flew by with us just talking, watching TV, and comforting one another. I wasn't allowed to sleep over with him, so I had to leave him at the hospital to have more tests done to find out why he was so confused.

The next day, when I went to see him, his face was much better. He smiled at me, which he had not done for a long time, and told me I looked beautiful. I felt all the butterflies and couldn't stop smiling. I had my natural hair out that day, which was always his favourite on me. That day, he was able to better hold a conversation with me, and I noticed that the swelling of the tumour on his head had decreased. Having already been in hospital for two days, he seemed to be doing much better.

The doctor told us João would need to stay another night so they could monitor him and make sure he was doing better. João was not happy at all, but I, on the other hand, felt a little content because I could see how much he was already improving.

The following day, I went to the hospital around 11 a.m. with bags full of his favourite fruit and water so I could see João and also have some time to speak to the doctor when she came to see him. I was about to go into the room to see my husband when a nurse came over to tell me I wasn't allowed to go in due to the fact that it was outside of their visiting hours. A colleague of hers handed me a permission slip that was necessary if I wanted to see him before 2 p.m. as required by company policy.

I pleaded to at least be able to take the fruit to his room so he could know I was there and have some of his favourite things. She let me in for a brief moment. The second I left his room, I called my daughter and cried.

I hung up on my daughter and talked to the nurse, as I thought it was she who didn't want to let me in, even though all the other nurses always let me in. She was next to another colleague who asked her to call the manager to talk to me. She took me to a room to wait for the manager. The same nurse came back to see me, and she told me that the manager would let me in today and tomorrow at any time so I could see my husband, and if I wanted, I could go in now.

I started talking to the nurse about everything that was hurting me. I told her that I didn't come to the hospital to spend the whole day there, as I had to pick up my children from school. I explained that the hospital was so far from my house, and I had to pay a lot of money to come to see my husband, and the money was already short. I asked her if she thought it was fair for someone to go through all of this, to come to the hospital to see her husband, who had a tumour on his head and be turned away.

I was in tears as I explained everything to her. It felt like I had a giant ball stuck in my throat.

She apologised and told me she was just following hospital rules, but that I could come in and see him now. I told her that it didn't make a difference because I had gone to the hospital to talk to the doctors so they could tell me anything regarding my husband's condition, as he wasn't in the best state. I had to find out through my daughter on the phone that he was no longer in his room, either; the doctor had taken him to do a skin biopsy as they believed they had found a tumour on his back and needed to confirm if it was the same type of cancer.

I wished the nurse goodbye and started making my way home, calling my friend in the meantime so I could vent to her. I told her everything that had occurred, and she gave me strength. I heard her weep on the phone, and our tears fell in unison. She tried to make me feel better by inviting me to come over to have a coffee with her, but I had to pass. I genuinely wasn't in the best of moods, and I knew I would not be good company.

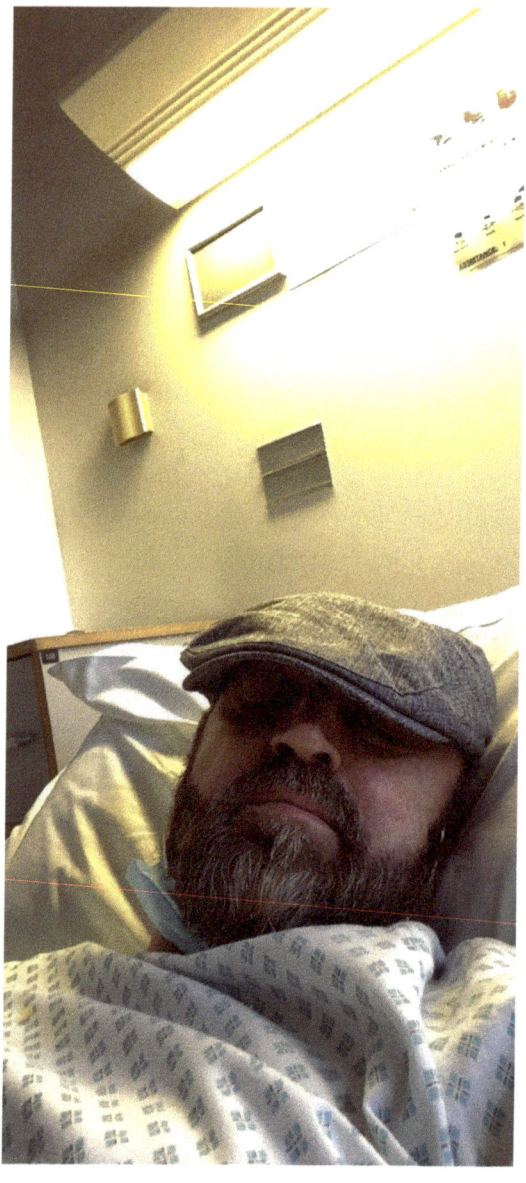

CHAPTER 12

TIME AFTER TIME

I hung up the phone and took the bus home, thinking about my children, who I would be picking up from school, and their faces if they saw how sad their mum was and all the questions they would have.

My little ones still had no clue their dad had cancer, but they were aware that he was unwell. The last thing I wanted was for them to carry our pain and suffering. I wanted them to have the best day possible, so I headed to the shop to quickly buy all of their favourite snacks and the ingredients to make my son, João Carlos, his favourite food. It is a traditional dish from Angola called *moamba de ginguba*, chicken and okra marinated in peanut butter. I got home and started cooking right away as it was nearing the time I had to pick them up from school, and I knew they would be really hungry. I cooked, and the house smelled divine, so I sat and ate my feelings away.

At 3 p.m., I started making my way to pick up my kids from school, putting on a fake smile so they wouldn't see how much pain I was in. As soon as I opened the door to our house, Camilla said it smelt really good. My son immediately recognised the smell and did a little happy dance as he knew straight away what the meal was. His innocence and sheer happiness made me giggle. Seeing them happy made me happy, and I would do anything and everything to keep that smile on their faces.

Despite how tired I was, I suggested we all watch a movie together in my bed, and Camilla ran upstairs immediately, but João Carlos said he wanted to play with his friends on the PS4. I couldn't be mad as I wanted him to relax and have fun, so Camilla and I cuddled up in bed to watch a movie, and I just completely dozed off.

About an hour or so had passed before I woke up. I knew there was one more thing I could do to make them smile, so I said, 'Who wants waffles?' and they perked up and started shouting, 'Me! Me! I want waffles!' I was their favourite, and they scarfed it down without hesitation.

Throughout the day, I kept in contact with my husband and the doctors so I could check how he was doing, and we video-chatted when possible. His strength to carry on was the only thing pushing me forward, too, and I knew I had to be strong for my children.

Every morning before I dropped them off at school, I always told them, 'Try your best today. Even if it feels like you're having a bad day, put your best feet forward.' I'd had a horrible day, but I told myself, 'Helena, try to make it a good day,' and that's what I did.

It was a Friday, and since the kids didn't have school the next day, we were watching a movie when I received a call from the hospital saying João was being discharged from the hospital tomorrow. I was beyond happy.

My sister came over the next morning to help me clean the house whilst my friend's husband and João's good friend went to pick him up from the hospital. Once the house was all clean and ready for his arrival, my sister took my children for a quick walk while my friends and I waited at home for the hospital to call me so we could go to collect him. I wanted to see if he was ready, so I called him on FaceTime and saw that he was already outside the hospital, waiting for us. My friends and I couldn't believe it. João definitely didn't like hospitals.

We drove as fast as possible to pick him up. I wish I could have framed his smile when he arrived home. I could tell he had missed it and his family.

Our friends stayed with us for a while, chatting away, and then went home. João and I finally had some alone time, and my heart was full again, seeing how happy he was to be home, knowing that he would start doing chemo again. It would be his seventh session, and it would begin again in a week, so we were happy that things were back on track.

Following the results of his exams, we were told there was no cancer in the liver nor in the bowel, just in his head.

CHAPTER 13

LOSING MY MIND

*B*ut there was one thing the doctors hadn't told us. There was cancer in his bones. They knew it was there and were monitoring it, and it had shrunk. He reassured us that the chemo was working well, and we believed him, as João seemed to be doing much better. We even noticed that his hair was slowly growing back in.

We continued the fight, hoping and praying that João would receive a miracle and be cured of cancer. We wanted to celebrate him as a cancer survivor. December 2021 would mark three years since he was first diagnosed with cancer. We have always been thankful that we got to have those three years with him, but I knew how tired he was of his battle. We will always thank God for my husband's life. For better or worse, he continued at our side, and we hoped it would continue for many years. By the grace of God, we prayed he would be healed.

December 2021 marked three years since he'd been diagnosed, and during that time, João experienced a lot of body aches. He wasn't able to sleep properly, and he kept tossing and turning at night. He continued to do chemotherapy, but the tumour in his head continued to grow.

He had an appointment with oncology, and I went with João for support, of course, but also to record the appointments so both Jessica and Catarina could hear what was going on when they couldn't be there physically. As soon as we walked into the appointment, João told the doctor that he was ready to hear it, and the doctor seemed confused. João wanted to hear that he didn't have any time left to live.

The doctor, however, said something else, that there was a drug out there that cost £600 a month that could help João have a better quality of life with cancer. The doctor knew of this drug, but he never told us about it because he didn't know what our financial situation was.

Let me begin by saying how wrong it was to rob someone of time, to rob someone of a better quality of life without even mentioning it to us. As I said, I would do anything for my family, and my family would do the same; if we had known about this drug earlier, we would have done everything in our power to make sure João had it. If he had told us about it earlier, João would have been better, and his condition would have got better.

I was devastated by this news, but João looked calm. After his PET scan on our way home, I asked João why he said he was ready to receive the bad news, and he said that he was just simply tired of the disease. Imagine how much pain you have to be in that you would rather hear, 'You don't have much time left' instead of battling the disease that's killing you.

Christmas came around, and we spent it in harmony, having our favourite meals, singing songs, and spending time with each other. João's pain worsened, however, and we thought it was best for him to go to the hospital to make sure everything was okay. On 31 December, we noticed that João was a lot more confused than usual, so Catarina drove him to the hospital, and for the first time in the twenty-three years since we had Catarina, the family wasn't together to celebrate New Year. We facetimed each other at midnight. Catarina and João wished us a happy new year whilst the little ones cheered back, and Jessica and I cried at the thought of us being away from them.

João spent three nights in the hospital, and due to COVID regulations, I wasn't allowed to see him.

By day four, João came home, and we were so happy to have him back, but he was still in so much pain that I genuinely didn't understand how they could discharge him. I immediately called João's oncology team and told them what was happening, and João had to be taken to another hospital to have more exams done. I felt so drained, and I couldn't believe it was happening all over again for what felt like the millionth time.

The next day, I woke up really early and went to the hospital to see João with my Brazilian friend. When we arrived, we were told he had been transferred to another hospital so they could perform an emergency operation. I was shocked. No one had informed me about this, and I began shaking, thinking about my poor husband. I hadn't even eaten anything that morning, but I felt the urge to throw up, scream, and cry.

I received a call from the hospital a few minutes later, requesting my permission as his wife so João could have the operation on his head. I could not make decisions, let alone that one. I kept replaying the doctor's words in my head, all of the risks he was facing, and I couldn't decide, but João was at the doctor's side, and he wanted to know what I thought was best. How could I make such a life-altering decision on his behalf? What if he never talked again? What if he never walked again? What if he never made it out of that operating room?

I included my daughters in the call so they could help me make the decision, and they agreed that if it was the best option for their father, we would allow the surgery to take place.

And that was that.

The doctor let us know it would be taking place that same day. I just prayed that everything would go well. At home, my daughters prayed. When I got home, I prayed over and over again.

The hospital called me later to let me know that they wouldn't be doing the operation that day, but they wanted me to come in to speak to them the next day. Another disappointment. Another heartbreak. My world shattered again.

I went to bed and woke up around 4 a.m., racking my brain as to why the doctors needed to speak to me, and I just knew they had found something else.

The number thirteen had been present in our lives too often, from the day João was diagnosed to that day; the 13th of January 2022 was when everything had changed. The 13th of January was when I walked in to find my husband laying in a hospital bed in so much pain. The 13th of January was when we went into that meeting and were told that my husband, João, had very little time to live.

He had four to eight weeks left to live with no treatment options left. The tumour in his head had doubled in size, and the operation was no longer an option. If they operated on him, he would never walk or talk again, and his life as he knew it would cease to exist.

I couldn't believe what I was hearing. I had always accepted that João had cancer, but I always hoped he would be cured. I had faith in that miracle. I prayed so much that I would have my husband again, but it wasn't possible. I didn't see João's face when he received the news, and I don't remember how he reacted. Because the world slowed down, faces blurred, and voices silenced, and all that could be heard was me crying. I cried so much in front of those doctors, in front of my João.

All I heard was his voice, telling me to 'Calm down.' My husband had just been told he had weeks left to live, and somehow, he was comforting me. He was my calm, my haven, an absolutely incredible man. He had received the worst news of his life, and yet there he was, making sure that I was okay. That was all he wanted, to make sure his family would be okay.

The doctor told me he would have to stay that day and be discharged the next day. I didn't know how to function, how I could go home and leave my husband alone in the hospital after he'd received the worst news possible.

We called Catarina and Jessica and told them what the doctors had said, and I had never seen two people cry that quickly. It was horrible to see their reactions, to see them coming to accept that their dad was dying.

I left the hospital and prayed all the way home, saying that with God, nothing was impossible. How would my little ones react? How could I possibly tell them their dad would die soon? I don't remember how we spent the rest of the day; I just know that I cried all of the tears I had in my system. I felt numb. I felt as if someone had taken my heart out and stomped on it. I was so angry with the world and the doctors who had failed my husband and robbed him of his life.

CHAPTER 14

LOSING THE POWER TO WALK

The next day, João came home, and he was more confused, doing and saying things without explanation. I told him it was time to tell his family, and he asked me not to say anything, but I knew I had to, so I called them without him knowing. I told them everything that had been happening and the news we had received, and I felt so bad because his parents were elderly, and they lived all the way in Portugal. They just cried and screamed and said they wanted to come to the UK to see him and spend time with their son.

João eventually found out and was upset because I'd told his family, but I knew he just didn't want to worry them. I would have felt so guilty if his parents had not been able to spend some time with him before he passed away, so I knew it was the right thing to do.

Nurses came in and out of our house, doing routine checks on João. One time, a nurse asked João how he was feeling with all that was happening, and João said he didn't feel anything and that all he wanted was to die in peace. The nurse went on to ask him if when he was dying, he wished to be resuscitated, and he immediately said no.

That's when we all realised: João had been preparing for this for days, weeks, months, and years. He had accepted that he would not be cured and his illness would eventually kill him. It was why he was always calm. It was why he always told us not to worry. It was why he always awaited bad news because it was what he wanted. He wanted—needed—to be free of all the pain and suffering he felt. How a human could prepare for their own death was beyond me. I would never understand all the thoughts in his head. I would never know all the times he cried by himself at the thought of leaving us behind. I would never understand why it was my husband.

God always has a plan, and I have full faith in Him, but at that moment, we all questioned why. My daughters and I hated being in that room, listening to those questions, and hearing what João thought of everything was horrible. We always left his room crying, even though we tried our best not to cry around him.

A few days went by, and his bodily pain had worsened to the point where he was unable to walk or simply get up to go to the bathroom. When the nurse came over, she panicked and called the ambulance to take him to the hospital so tests could be done to check if he now had pancreatic cancer.

Two men arrived with a wheelchair, gave him nitrous oxide to relieve the pain, and they carried him down the stairs from our bedroom and into the ambulance. When

João and I arrived at the hospital, they took us to a room, and a doctor arrived to let us know that his cancer was already so advanced that nothing could be done for him. He prescribed João some medication since he was in so much pain, and the hospital prepared to transport him back to our home.

Since João was very weak and unable to walk, Catarina and I had his arms around our shoulders, and we carried him into the kitchen. Jessica was in the kitchen with him when he said that he could walk by himself and tried to stand up, but he fell, and his knee started bleeding. To this day, Jessica says it was such a traumatic sight, seeing her dad collapse like that, his own legs giving out on him as he had no strength to walk. I remember her screaming, 'Help! Somebody help! Dad fell! Please!'

I ran downstairs to find him on the floor with Jessica crouched over him, crying and trying to help him up.

We managed to lift him up and sit him back down. All Jessica could say was, 'Why, Dad? I told you not to stand up. You broke my heart,' when she saw the blood on his leg. It was such a horrible experience, but unfortunately, it wasn't the only incident.

The ambulance had brought him down the stairs, but they couldn't bring him back up to our room. Catarina and I at first tried to carry him up the stairs, but it wasn't possible, so he sat on the stairs and pulled himself up to our 'Hep,' step-by-step. It was horrible to see him like that. I wouldn't wish it on anyone, having to see someone you love in so much pain, so weak they have to lift themselves up the stairs like that.

Since that day, João was unable to walk.

One day, I was preparing the bathtub so he could have a nice relaxing bath. I put in his favourite bath salts and made it all comfy for him. I had to help him out of bed and into the bath, dragging him slowly until he managed to get in. I cried so much during the process because it pained me to see him like that.

He stayed in the bath, relaxing while I cleaned our room. When it was time to get him out of the bathtub, I realised how hard it would be. I got him up, but taking his legs out of the bathtub took forever, as I didn't want to cause him any more pain. I took one leg out, but when I tried to get the other leg out, we both fell on that bathroom floor. I did my best to minimise his impact, but I couldn't. I hit my head on the bathroom heater and managed to scratch his chest, trying to hold him.

Those seconds we were on the floor were horrible. I asked if he was okay, and even though he was in so much pain and on the floor with me, he asked if I was okay. God had given me the biggest blessing in João.

Jessica ran upstairs frantically when she heard the thud to find us both lying on the bathroom floor, and she panicked.

Since João was naked, I told her to wait outside the bathroom door whilst I got up and lifted him up, but I couldn't. João was only able to crawl at that point, so he did. That image of him crawling like a baby so slowly to our room broke my heart. I couldn't stop crying, but João just kept telling me that he was okay, and I needed to stop crying. He has always been like that. He hated seeing me upset.

He was kneeling in our room, and I dressed him the way he was, kneeling on the floor. I managed to put him in bed. It was difficult, but I did it.

I told myself he'd better not go to the bathroom to shower anymore.

João's parents arrived from Portugal with João's favourite uncle and younger brother. They planned to return the following Monday. João was so happy to see everyone. He talked to everyone, but he just couldn't walk. He ate alone without needing anyone to help him, and he still drank his wine. I always had meals with him in our room because I always wanted to be by his side. He would lay in bed with me and the little ones, and our daughters, Catarina and Jessica, would lay on the floor next to him so we could all watch movies together, our favourite tradition. Although we couldn't watch them downstairs anymore, we made do with our bedroom, and it felt really nice to have those family moments.

João's parents were due to return on Monday, but I told them it would be better for them to stay a little longer with their son, so they stayed.

João's pain started to get worse. He was unable to get up and walk or even go to the bathroom, so we decided it would be a better option to get him diapers. That way, we could ease some of the pain he was feeling and not put any strain on his body by lifting him up to go to the toilet.

Weeks had gone by since João was told he had little time left to live, and by then, he could no longer speak. He had no strength in his arms or body, so I had to feed him. When he was no longer able to physically turn himself over in bed, I had to turn him so he could feel more comfortable.

He ate very little and started to lose so much weight; his legs were so thin, and I could barely recognise my husband. Having to change his diapers was such a strange feeling; I couldn't believe what I was doing. My husband, who had once been so full of life and energy, the best man I have ever met in this world, now had to have his diapers changed by me. I knew he felt ashamed or sad seeing me change him as he didn't want to see me in that position, and I felt so bad thinking about how he must have felt, knowing he could no longer do it himself. I would tell him, 'It's me, Helena, your love', and he would just look at me sadly. I would tell him, 'It's okay. Let me take care of you.'

CHAPTER 15

HALLUCINATION

*T*hirteen followed us everywhere. On the *13th of February*, João was not well at all. He was no longer eating, and he wasn't breathing properly, and we all panicked because we thought he was going to pass away. I called my sister, and she came straightaway. We all kneeled around the bed he was lying in and prayed for a miracle.

My mother-in-law just cried at the sight of her son. I said to myself, if João dies today, on the *13th of February*, it is not God's plan; it is some evil force following us.

My sister was helping me change his position on the bed when I called the nurse, who came over as quickly as possible to give João an emergency injection. They said it could make him agitated and that he could also hallucinate, but I reassured her that if it was the best option for him, we were happy for him to have it.

By nighttime, João was a little more responsive, and he began talking. He was confused from the medication and started saying, 'Tomorrow, let's go for a walk. Where do you want to go tomorrow?' and then he would switch the conversation and say, 'We're going to have sex tomorrow,' and he lifted the sheets like he always did to see if I was wearing sexy underwear or not. He ran his hands along my legs and bum like he always did. He knew I always felt cold on my back, so he pulled the sheets to cover me. I knew he was my husband, even if his physical appearance had changed.

That night, I couldn't sleep because João was hallucinating a lot. He would try to get up to go to the bathroom even though he couldn't. He spent the whole night moving everything on his bedside table around, and he always cleaned the sheets even though they were already clean. He was hallucinating things that didn't exist. I was exhausted since I didn't sleep nights, but I felt so bad for him because he had no control over his actions because of the medication.

I promised our children that we would go ice skating the next day, and I had already paid, but all I wanted was to cancel with the kids. I was super tired, but I looked at their faces and saw how much they needed to have some fun, too.

I went with Camilla and João Carlos, while Jessica and Catarina looked after João. We went ice skating and had some lunch, too. Just seeing my little ones so happy made me so happy, too.

Ever since João had the injection, he was not the same. He ate very little, and we fed him small amounts through a syringe. The nurse came over to see João and talk to us. When she looked at João, her face changed. She asked how long he had been like that, and we realised she was very worried about him.

She called my daughters and me into the kitchen, but Catarina didn't want to come to listen to the conversation. Today, I look back at that day and see why she didn't want to hear what she already knew.

When the nurse started talking to Jessica and me, she said João was very bad and that this could be João's last week. I couldn't believe what she was saying. Jessica started crying, and so did I. The nurse said she would be back in a few days to see how things were, but she didn't show up anymore.

On Wednesday, February 23rd, João couldn't eat anymore. He didn't even drink some water. He wasn't talking; he just slept. He was really bad.

My friend came to pray with everyone, but João wasn't responsive. All he did was sleep. There were around seven of us in the room, and I noticed he had peed, so I ordered everyone out of the room so I could change him. Everyone left, and I closed the door and cleaned and changed him while he slept. I laid my head on my husband's chest so I could smell his scent that I loved so much and told him how much I loved him and that he smelled so good. I laid like that on his chest for another minute, and when I looked up, I saw his beautiful blue eyes looking at me.

He was awake!

I asked him, 'Baby, do you love me?'

He replied, 'Don't you know that? Yes,' his usual response.

I shouted to everyone, 'He's awake!' and they all came.

My daughters ran into the room. They were so happy.

João looked at them with so much love and adoration, and it was the first time in weeks that he hadn't been confused. At that moment, he clearly recognised everyone. We pointed at each other and asked him our names. When he got it right, we jumped, cried, and laughed.

João had awakened to life that Wednesday. This João laughed with everyone, talked to everyone in the room, and even ate some soup and drank some water. Everyone told him how much they loved him, and João slept through the night peacefully.

On Thursday, João's best friend, Victor, came. Victor didn't even know João had cancer because João had never said anything to him. When I told him, he didn't want to believe it.

He cried when he saw João in that state, that super handsome man who now had a different appearance. He no longer looked like my husband; his face was different.

João looked at his friend, listening to what he said, but the João on Wednesday, the João from the night before, was not the same João on Thursday. The one on Thursday never spoke again.

CHAPTER 16

THE ROAD TO THE END

Friday, February 25th 2022 — the end.
Ever since João was told he had weeks left to live, he had stayed upstairs, in our bed., but the nurses had promised us the equipment so we could get him out of bed. It would enable him to get up, go into the garden, and enjoy the sun, something he hadn't been able to do in forty-three days.

That Friday, the hospital equipment had arrived that would enable him to have a better life, but he would never get to use it. They also brought a hospital bed, which they put in our living room. We were waiting for the ambulance to come with the men so they could move him downstairs.

Whilst Jessica and I made space for the bed downstairs, Catarina was upstairs, taking care of her father, cleaning him and brushing his teeth. By that point, he was neither eating nor drinking and was breathing very poorly.

I had a dentist appointment that day, and I ran there, but I still arrived late. They made me reschedule for one month's time, despite my having waited a month for this one. I was already frustrated and upset, but I decided that since I was out, I would buy the donuts my children liked, and I stopped by a supermarket to buy sushi for us to eat.

A sadness came over me; João loved sushi, but he wouldn't be able to eat it, so I called Catarina crying, saying, 'I'm going to lose my husband. He will leave me, and I will be alone.'

She told me to stop crying, and that Dad was okay.

I hung up the phone and made my way home, crying so much on the bus. I made an Instagram story telling our followers how I felt, and I remember saying that I was going to lose my husband.

When I got home, my daughter, Jessica, was with her best friend, Agne, and my in-laws were eating, and I noticed that he still hadn't been brought down, so I went upstairs to check on him. When I walked into our room, I was frightened—the João I had left that morning looked so different. His blue eyes were open, but he was breathing very poorly; his whole body strained when he tried to breathe, and I was filled with fear.

Catarina was next to him, and Jessica came upstairs. They told him how much they loved him, and Jessica went back downstairs crying. It was hard for her to see her dad like that, and it triggered her, and she cried a lot. Catarina was stronger. She cried, but since she had experience as a carer, she knew how to take care of her dad, for which I was grateful.

João's uncles were coming from Portugal. They would land around 7 p.m. I talked to João and told him that he needed to wait for his uncles. I don't know why I said that, but I had the feeling he was dying. I told him again, 'My love, wait for your uncles. They are on their way.'

The men arrived to carry João downstairs, and we were so happy to finally have him down in the living room, but his breathing was getting worse. My mother-in-law just cried. I sat next to João, singing to him and holding his chest. We sang Anderson Freire's song, '*Acalma o meu coracao*', a song that had gotten my family through all of our hardships.

The whole family came together, holding hands and praying over his hospital bed because we all knew it was time. João's uncles arrived with their daughters around 8.35 pm, and the moment they saw the state João was in, they began to cry. They spoke to him for about ten minutes, and it seemed as though João was listening because his eyes followed his uncles.

At around 8.50 p.m., João started rolling his eyes and foaming at the mouth. My husband was dying. João was dying. He was waiting for his uncles so he could die peacefully. The house was filled with screaming, deep guttural screams and loud cries. All I heard was Jessica asking her friend, Agne, to take João Carlos and Camilla out of the room on a walk, so they didn't have to see their dad pass away.

On Friday, February 25th, 2022, at approximately 8.53 p.m., I lost the love of my life. My children lost their father. My in-laws lost their son. João's uncles lost their beloved nephew. The world lost a hero, but heaven gained the most amazing angel.

The situation was dire. Suffering was all around us. I contacted my sister as soon as it happened as I needed her, and I knew she would like to say her goodbyes as well. My daughter, Catarina, urged me to call Kelly as well.

I called everyone, including my uncle Clemente, who had known João for years, and as soon as I told him, he panicked and rushed out of the house. Before I knew it, my house was packed with people, including those I hadn't seen in years. That's the thing about death: it brings people together under the most treacherous of situations.

We contacted the ambulance to say that João had died so they could come to collect the body, and they advised us to reach out to a funeral home so they could handle his funeral arrangements. We weren't prepared for any of that. As much as João had urged us to prepare ourselves, we never lost hope that he would recover.

We didn't have any funeral homes in mind, but my daughter, Jessica, kneeled next to his body as she looked for some near us. We called, and they arrived to take his body. I didn't want to see it. I didn't want to see them carry my husband out on a stretcher, covered in a black bag.

Kelly and a cousin of mine took me outside so I could get some fresh air. I had all of my family calling, nieces and siblings from Portugal, and it felt as if I could not breathe. Kelly and my sister took me to the bedroom, and they changed the sheets on my bed so I could lie down. Still, I couldn't believe João was dead.

My daughters were downstairs saying their goodbyes, kissing his forehead, and telling him how much they loved him. Catarina took off the bracelets he was wearing, and Jessica covered her ears so she wouldn't overhear the people moving his body onto the stretcher, so she wouldn't hear them zipping the black bag with her dad inside.

I jumped out of bed when I heard more screaming, and I screamed for my husband as I tried to run downstairs, but someone was holding me so I wouldn't go down the stairs.

That night was a blur, a memory I have tried to erase. I don't know who held me on that day, but I'm grateful they did, as I was so weak, and I could have collapsed down those stairs. As I sat on the stairs, I saw them wheel him out of the living room and out the door in a black bag. All I could do was shout and cry, 'My husband!'

My daughters walked after him, and I heard them screaming out for their dad whilst my uncle Clemente tried to comfort them.

They took me to bed again.

My daughter, Jessica, called her friend, Agne, to ask if my little ones were okay. She asked if they had a clue what was happening, and Agne said, 'They're okay. I took them on a walk and to the shop so they could buy their favourite snacks.' I was so grateful for her. Because of her and Jessica's quick thinking, my kids didn't have to see that traumatic experience.

I lay down in my bed and texted my friends, Catia and Laudilena, to tell them the news. They wanted to come to see me then, but I said, 'Not today.' They came the following morning.

I don't remember the rest of the night; I just know that everyone went to bed crying, praying to God that he would watch over João, praying that João was now resting peacefully.

João's uncles and my in-laws were scheduled to return to Portugal on Monday, so we arranged with the funeral home to go on Monday to view João's body.

The days passed by painfully slowly. We lit candles, sang him songs, and just leaned on each other for support. It was so pleasant to have everyone around.

Monday came around, and we made our way to visit João. When we entered, my mother-in-law almost fainted. We asked them to cover João, as the thought of seeing him would be unbearable. It was difficult for everyone to see his dead body.

João's family returned to Portugal. Now, there were only five of us at home. Our man, our king, was no longer with us.

CHAPTER 17

GOODBYE

The next day, we all gathered to take care of João's funeral, trying to give him the finest send-off possible. We chose everything in detail. We chose the colour blue because it was João's favourite colour, and we didn't want too many flowers. João and I always said that we didn't think it was right for a dead person to receive so many flowers. A person who had already died wouldn't see any of those things, so we decided to spend it on other things.

João called himself 'Lord Vilar', so we ordered flowers spelling 'Lord Vilar' in white and blue to go on the hearse. We had beautiful white horses and chose some of his favourite songs. It was all very beautiful. Despite the hardship, we were so grateful for everyone's support.

When we found out that João was terminally ill, we created a GoFundMe page, and so many people donated. We used some of the money to pay for treatments and buy machines to help him, though it was futile. The money we had leftover enabled us to pay for his funeral, and we couldn't be more grateful to everyone who donated. Because of you, we got to lay João to rest in the most beautiful way. In England, funerals work differently. Whilst many countries bury people within a few days, everything here is very time-consuming, and it can take up to months before they are buried. We wanted to make sure it was on a Friday, which just so happened to fall on the 18th of March. It felt so meaningful, as João's birthday was on the 18th of November. I love numbers, so the coincidence of it almost felt like fate.

A lot of people came from Portugal for João's funeral—he had many friends—but we insisted on inviting only the people João loved the most. My daughters and I wanted a private ceremony. I had to be mentally okay to think about who would carry João's coffin and the songs to be played. Someone who had lost her love now had to decide how to say goodbye to him. It was difficult, but thank God I had my daughters at my side, who helped me with all the details of the funeral.

The 18th arrived, the day I would see my husband for the last time. The funeral home informed me that we had to go early to see the body because once they closed the coffin it could no longer be opened. I prepared a beautiful outfit for João in his style, the way he loved to wear it. I put his perfume on my clothes so I could smell him for the last time. I dressed in the boots I loved to see him wear.

My daughters wrote lengthy letters to their father, and I gathered everything I wrote—our laws—that had been hanging in our house for years; it was time for my daughters and me to go in to see João.

The lady warned us that when we entered that we should not look at the coffin right away, but that we should go in and take a breath before looking inside, so that's what we did. My children saw their father's body first—I was afraid to look; I couldn't look. I wanted to, but the pain stopped me.

My children cried a lot. My little ones reacted very badly, so I approached the coffin to comfort the kids when I saw the face of my man, my husband. I remember being cold. I couldn't feel my legs. When I saw João's face, I couldn't believe that the person who was lying there looked like my husband, but it wasn't João. That face didn't belong to my man. I thought I would see my husband's face that day, all beautiful like he was always. I never thought I would see the face of the man who had suffered for three years. The man who died next to me was not my husband; he was someone else.

The image I had of João dying next to me was traumatic. He looked like a skull. His face was so thin, and he had no beard. I had this image in my head, and I remember telling my daughters, and they told me they had the same image of the same man in their minds.

He lay there, cold, with his beard and his beautiful hair. When I went closer to see my man, I wished I could have smelled his scent, but I didn't. The body didn't smell like João. He was all dressed up but without his shoes, because I think they couldn't put them on. I couldn't touch him. My hands were trembling.

My children cried and touched their father. The image of seeing my children suffering broke my heart. How could this have happened to my family? My children always loved their father, and João always loved his children madly, but now he'd lost his children and the woman he loved so much. We missed him so much.

I hugged my youngest children and told them that their father was now an angel, and he would always be there to protect us. A lot of people said that João died first to protect the family he loved so much, and that is the reason I'm holding on to. That is what I want to believe.

I cried as I knelt near the coffin. I didn't even notice the moment people walked in to see João, but when I got up, I looked back, and the room was full of people. There were João's uncles, my uncles, my nieces, my sister, and many friends. When I looked at everyone, I had such a big pain in my chest because everyone who was there loved João a lot. There could have been more people there, but some were far away and couldn't attend. It hurt that some people we considered family did not show up. There were friends we'd had for ten years who turned their back on us.

I'd called them when I found out that João had two months left to live. I remember telling them they should come over to give João a hug and that he would be very happy to see them. She agreed, but she never came, and I didn't hear from them again. Her husband, who said João was his brother, never came to see him. These were the same friends we did everything together with; we went out to dinner, to the movies, clubbing and even took vacations together. Jessica and I babysat their children and watched them grow up. They came to every party we threw. They were our neighbours and my children's friends. Before I told them the news, they checked in on him. When he had his operation, they had gone to see João at the hospital, and they would have parties to cheer João up when he felt a little better. I couldn't understand why they disappeared from João's life at the moment when he needed them the most. When my family needed their support the most, the people who knew how we'd suffered turned their backs on us.

João asked about them, but they didn't seem to care. I didn't know how to tell my husband, who was already suffering, that people we considered family didn't care about us. I wondered how it could be possible that there were people like that in the world.

Today, I can say that it was their loss. They lost out on our friendship because I know how amazing we are and how warm and friendly we are with our friends. I'm very loyal, and I'm faithful to my friends and family. Life has taught me that sometimes our friends are worth as much as family. I help so many people, and I am met with ingratitude.

My being on social media bothers a lot of people. It bothered my family and friends. I had a sister who sent me a message telling me that I thought I was better than everyone. She told me that I was unloved and I would die alone. At a time when I was already suffering, she said everything she knew would hurt me deeply, and it did.

This all happened because I didn't get involved in the family drama. They were discussing issues in the group chat that had nothing to do with me. I didn't involve myself, so they spoke badly about me, wishing the most horrible things on me. Everything that happened to me, I just handed it over to—and trusted in—God. How could a sister wish something so evil on me? How could a friend of a decade turn her back on me when I needed her the most? I live my life, not my problems, as I have said many times. I never stopped smiling or showing my face on social media. Even though I suffered so much inside, I continued smiling and laughing.

I blocked out everyone who made me suffer. I put them out of my life forever, including my sister. I have not spoken to her since, and I won't because anyone who talks to you the way she spoke to me is not a sister; they're an enemy. I received so much hate from my own flesh and blood for making videos. I only made videos because I enjoyed it. It became a way to relieve stress, and it made João and I smile when we were suffering.

Today, we have a lot of followers on all of our social media, and there are thousands of people who love my family and show it every day, and for my supporters, I am grateful. It is true that people can have everything in life, but if you have something they don't, they hate you for it. This is because they know they cannot compete with you. They didn't have my smile, my shine, or my strength to keep moving on. Your light comes from God. He gave you life, and He gives you your shine. Some sparkle more than others; I believe my husband and I did. It was only because of this that I was able to continue making videos, go out with friends, and laugh even though I was hurting.

God is everything in my life. I know God has always protected me, and it is only by His grace that I am still standing. It is true, God does not give you more than you can bear. We all have our cross. Some may be heavier than others, but God is always present in our lives. God is great, and it is with his grace that João was with his family for three years even though he had cancer.

Going back to the day of João's funeral, I was both happy and sad because a lot of people who were there had come to London for their first time, and it was for a funeral. If João were alive, he would be super-happy to see everyone in London. He was not present in the flesh, but he was present in spirit.

They came to close the coffin, and it was horrible. His body was entombed in a beautiful white coffin. His wake was touching, and we insisted on such a beautiful ceremony, one as beautiful as he had been. We released a white dove as a symbol, saying that João was now resting peacefully. We missed him so much.

CHAPTER 18

THE END OF OUR BEAUTIFUL LOVE STORY

I miss my husband all the time; when I go to bed, I sleep on my side of the bed, and I can't sleep in the whole bed because I feel like he's still in the bed. I often feel João's presence near me. I feel him touching me on the head regularly. The other day, I had an erotic dream about him—it had never happened when he was alive—and I don't know if I had the dream because I miss him. Sometimes, I can't believe João really died. I have days when it seems like I'm sleeping, and I'm going to wake up from the nightmare, and my life will continue as it always has, with João super-healthy, full of life, and full of dreams.

I swear, I get up many times, thinking he will come back, but a voice in my head reminds me that he has died, and I won't see him anymore. I will never be able to hug my husband again and smell his scent that I love so much. I will never be able to kiss him or touch his chest, play with his hair, or hold his hand whilst lying in bed watching movies. The voice wakes me up to reality every day and reminds me that what I had with João will never come back.

All of this hurts a lot. It is truly an indescribable pain. I don't like listening to his voice anymore because it makes me cry. I miss his smile. I miss the times we would be upset with each other, and we played little high school games and tried to avoid making eye contact. I miss yelling at him when he moved around in the bed whilst I was sleeping and he was getting up to go to work. I miss our Friday night tradition of sitting in the kitchen, eating shrimp. I miss going out to restaurants and ordering a bottle of wine for us to drink. I miss going out for dates and having to order for us since he always chose the worst dishes on the menu. I miss laughing with him. I miss everything I experienced with João. I miss the good and bad things.

João was a part of my life for over two decades. For over twenty-five years, I devoted myself to the man. We created four beautiful children together and built an empire. How can you lose a part of yourself, half of yourself, and still continue living?

Many think that just because I spend time with my friends or have a drink I have forgotten João, but that is impossible; I could never forget him. I close my eyes and see his face. I walk in the street and smell his perfume. I look at my four children and see half of him. I am simply learning to live without my other half.

There have been times when I was depressed, and I no longer had my husband there to make me feel better, and

I had to learn to get up alone. Today, I can say that I am discovering what it is to be alone again. Many have asked about what I have planned for the future, and the truth is that I'm still figuring it out. Everyone wants to know if I plan to stay single or if I will find someone else. The truth is that I've lived a truly romantic love story with my husband João. It was a fairytale to have been able to spend twenty-five years with him, to be able to say that I am João's wife, and these are the four beautiful children we created together.

The last five months before João left were torture for us. He suffered so much, and I am grateful that he is now resting peacefully. I suffered in ways I cannot describe. My kids suffered, too. We are simply just trying to stay alive, to find the strength in us to keep moving without having our hero around.

Those last months, I took care of João as he was my husband, and I did so until the day he took his last breath. If it was necessary, my family and I would have done so until eternity if it meant we could have him by our side, but that is being selfish. That would be inconsiderate of how he felt. He was in so much pain, and he was simply tired of having to fight every single day to stay alive. He wanted to be free. He needed to rest. We are slowly making peace with that.

I know that all he wants is for us to keep going, to keep on living and smiling. It is how he always was, telling us to go for walks to clear our heads and to go out to do things we enjoyed. I think a part of us felt guilty for doing those things when we knew he couldn't, but that is what love is, putting the other person above your own needs, wanting to see them happy even if you are in pain.

My story with João ended when he died, but I didn't. I am still alive, and I have a lot to keep breathing for; I have four children who need me.

Today, I can write this book and tell you that I am not looking for a man; I simply want to enjoy life. I want to travel to new places, make new friends, and do things I never thought of doing. If one day I fall in love again, it will be a bonus, a blessing, because everything that happens in my life is the work of God. If God decides I deserve to be happy again, I will lift my hands up to the sky and say thank you because the unfiltered truth is that no matter how hard I try, I will never find another man like João , a man who loved me so intensely, who was willing to love me in spite of all of my flaws and give me four beautiful blessings, a man who put his shyness aside to create videos on social media when I asked, a man so caring, selfless, and protective.

During our wedding ceremony, we vowed to love each other until death do us part, and that is what happened, but I will never be able to replicate the love we had for one another. Having gone through this whole experience with João just made me reflect more on life and what I want out of it. I tell everyone around me to enjoy life and experience everything whilst you still can, because you never know when it could all vanish.

We still have thousands of followers who know us, who have given us love and support and pushed me to write this book, people who have allowed me to be vulnerable and share our story. Unfortunately, I can't end this book with a happy ending due to João's passing away, but I can end it on a positive note: I have a good feeling about the future and what is in store for my family.

There is no future without a past, and although it didn't end the way I wanted it to, I have lived a beautiful life, and it might only get better because, with God, all things are possible.

I wrote this book to talk about my husband's cancer and everything our family dealt with, but that was not what I initially wanted to write about. I wanted to write a book about love, and in some ways, I have. I have told a love story through my own experience. While this book is about our secret, I already had an idea of what it would be about, and I had the title prepared. Just know that this is a romance novel. This was not the ending I dreamt of writing when I started this book—I always had the hope that João would come out on top of the disease—but I really enjoyed putting our story out there for everyone to know, and I just thank you so much for reading. Thank you to everyone who was present during this whole process. Thank you for your prayers, donations, love, and being our friends at heart.

Thank you, João, for being this super-wonderful person. Thank you for loving me so much. Thank you for being the best father in the world for our children. Thank you for being a good son to your parents. Thank you for being a good brother, uncle, and friend. You will always be present in our hearts. Rest in peace, my love. God knows what He does, and I will always trust in God.

Thank you, João, for everything, for all the love, respect, loyalty, honesty, and much more. You are the one and only, and I will be forever grateful. I know that I will never be able to find someone like you; we are inseparably linked because our love is eternal. You love me, and I will love you forever.

Forever

The Love of My Life

EPILOGUE

TORN PIECES OF ME

After my husband was diagnosed with cancer, we never told our little ones. As a mother, I thought it best not to talk about cancer with them. They knew their father was sick, but they didn't know what the illness was. I didn't know how to go about explaining what cancer was to them. I always told them that their father was sick and needed to have some operations, and it already pained them. They were both so sad.

I said that we now had to pray more so God could heal their father and he could get better. The kids were determined to pray. I thought it was so beautiful, these little humans so loaded with faith and believing that with God, nothing is impossible. This situation was hard enough to navigate but being a mother and a wife made it more difficult.

João and I were at a period of our lives where we could enjoy it. Our oldest daughters were already grown, and we could go out with friends, knowing our little ones were being cared for.

We started travelling, just the two of us. We went out at night more often on dates and even went out to bars and clubs. We started to enjoy our life more. Our love got stronger with each day that passed.

When this news came to our family, everything changed. I now had to bathe my husband. I now had to take care of my husband as if he were my son. I felt heartbroken seeing him in that condition. He lost more weight every day. There were days when he would get irate more easily because of his treatment, and he would yell at me without explanation. I cried.

I was suffocating. I was there for my family, and I had to take care of my husband and children—who was taking care of me? Who asked me how are you today? Who told me to rest and take a day off? I asked for help, but no one listened to me. I had to laugh when my heart was crying. I often wanted to disappear for a few days. When I thought about it, I would say to myself, 'If I disappear, what will become of my family? My children need me now more than ever. My husband needs me.' I looked at my family, and it was through them that I gained the strength to continue on this journey.

A lot of people asked me how I managed to smile in this situation. To me, it was important to live my life and not my problems.

I scheduled a meeting with my family, my children, and my husband. I talked about my being at home and how no one could see me, that I was there for everyone, but I felt alone. I told them it was getting hard for me. I understood

João's medication and treatment were making him not act like himself, but his yelling at me was hurting me too much, as all I wanted to do was take care of him. I talked about the possibility of my falling sick and how we would all fall apart. All I wanted was for us to unite more, pray more, and be there for each other. This formed the premise of the laws of the house. We wrote it on a piece of paper that we still have in our entryway today.

Everyone heard what I said and understood where I was coming from, and everything began to change little by little at home. When I said I wanted to disappear, it was to go anywhere for a week without a phone, anyplace where I could relax my head, a place that only existed in my head, a spa, a paradise, where I had everything I needed for me to get rid of my stress.

One day, João told me that he felt as if I no longer loved him, which wasn't true; I love João so much. He has been my best friend, lover, and companion for years. It would, however, be a blatant lie to say that our relationship hadn't changed due to our situation.

Intimacy was no longer a thought. It was hard to think about things like sex when we were dealing with this. I would tell him that when he was feeling better, we could have sex, that we were in no rush, and I just wanted him to be better. I never wanted him to feel as if he wasn't loved or he was robbing me of anything. I told him that sex was simply a bonus in our lives and he shouldn't worry about it because I knew him and the kind of man he was. I knew how our sex life had been, the number of times we'd had sex within those twenty-five years, and how hot it had been. Even if it wasn't now, it hadn't always been like that.

João and I had been together for twenty-five years. João was my best friend. It broke my heart to hear him think like that. Until you're in that situation, you don't understand. Your brain gets rewired. It doesn't even think about sex anymore. All it cares about is making sure your partner is taken care of.

I've cried a lot, and I still cry because sometimes, it's not easy to be Helena, who has often lost hope, whose screams for help few people understand. Helena, who gets up every day and goes to Instagram and wishes everyone a great day; she screams for help. When she gets up and says good morning to everyone because she wants to receive some of the love she transmits every day. Often, she receives your love, but other days, she doesn't.

Our followers are very important in my life, in our life. Because of you, I no longer feel the great loneliness I used to feel, but it is still there. Despite having a houseful of love from my husband and children, I felt lonely. I felt very alone. I do not know how to explain why I felt this loneliness. Maybe it was because I wanted to have someone like me in my life, someone I could tell everything I was going through without being judged. Human beings judge a lot, and it's hard to trust people these days. That's why I say, today and always, that my best friends are my family.

My children and my husband are my best friends. Every day I believe less in true friendships. I have friends; a lot of people know my friends. Thank God life taught me to be more trusting and find the good ones, friends to have a good time with. Friends who enjoy dancing, drinking, and laughing. I'm looking for a friend like me in this world.

Everyone judges. Everyone speaks. I don't want to have someone next to me that I trust with something, and an hour goes by, and the whole world knows about it. I need someone to listen. I felt lonely because my family was going through the same thing as me. We all experienced the same pain. It was hard to talk about my own problems because they didn't know how to help. They were struggling themselves. I wish I had someone with whom to share my pain, someone who really listened without judgement. I know I could have asked for psychological help, but I never did because I didn't want to talk about my life with strangers. I felt as if I only had my family, and my daughters were and are my best friends.

Let this be a lesson: if you know someone who is going through this situation or something similar, listen more, be more friendly, and judge less.

My Daughter Camilla's Chapter

Before everyone dives into Camilla's chapter, I want to say that she is a sweet girl with a pure heart who loves helping others. She is a sweet girl who loved her father very much. My daughter was ten years old when she wrote this mini book of hers. My husband was still alive and seeing me writing made her want to write what she was feeling, too. I confess that I haven't read what she's written. I am curious as a mother. I know this chapter will not be easy for anyone to read. Here my daughter shares what she experienced when she saw the father she loves so much suffering from an illness that would take his life. She knew her father was going to die. I hope this book can help many girls who are going through the same thing.

My Hero Dad

My dad, João Vilar, was diagnosed with this disease three years ago on December 13th. This is what changed our lives completely. Our lives have been such a struggle. Before all of this, my dad was a fun, typical dad. He was amazing. He was always up for challenges and would do anything for anyone.

Once we had discovered his illness, we always went to hospital nonstop for any and every treatment possible. It was tiring. My dad was getting worse every day. He had to go through radiotherapy, chemotherapy, MRIs, PET scans and more... But no matter what, we were always there for him. We all love my dad in many ways, and he knew that there were only such limited ways to show him.

Sometimes my dad was so sick that he would only be able to lay down and eat. The only thing that was benefiting him was walking. My dad would go for a walk outside every day typically with my dog (Cookie). I love my dad so much that not even words can describe.

Fast forwarding to 2021. Even though my dad was progressively getting weaker, he went out every day and enjoyed every moment. Christmas had just come around and everyone received amazing gifts. My mum had gifted me a gift I wanted for so long: an Apple Pen. This meant that the iPad was coming soon! The smile on my dad's face lit me up with joy to see he was as happy as me receiving this gift.

My dad was spoiled with tops, shoes, essentials, care, and more. To be honest, he deserved it for being an excellent dad. Sooner or later, something had started to catch my family's attention. We had started to realise there was something growing on the left side of my dad's head. And so, with discovering this, we had attempted to cover it up so no one could notice until we found out what it was. The bump had started to grow unbearably massive.

New Year arrived, but something was off. My dad wasn't there. My dad needed so much treatment, so we took him to the hospital. He was there for many days. My older sister, Catarina, was always there with my dad. Sometimes she would even sleep there. It came to a point where we were going to visit him as a family. The hospital didn't let us in...

We were devastated.

My sister all this time had to make up lousy excuses just to check up on him. The cries we had on New Year's Eve because my dad wasn't there to celebrate with us was horrendous. We all missed my dad deeply.

January had come, school started, and my dad was sadly still in hospital. But I managed to put that behind me and tried to have a good time. It was around the 11th -13th where everything had started to go deeply wrong. My family had got some news which had made them heartbroken. I didn't know about it since I was just a child. They had told everyone except for me and my brother, João Carlo). My sisters were very upset.

February

We had found out the massive bump on my dad's head was, in fact, a tumour. Oh boy... It was like the size of an orange. My sisters decided to make a gofundme page for my dad. We raised so much in just two hours of creating it. We were so thankful. All this money was going towards my dad because, of course, he deserved it.

My dad is my light, my happiness. More into February, my dad was getting weaker and weaker, to the point where he couldn't walk. He had to just stay in bed otherwise he would just develop more severe pain. Sometimes his mind would trick him into believing that he is still able to do things he can't. For example, go to the toilet. He couldn't walk so we had to give him adult absorbent pants.

Now we must feed him in bed. We even bought him fidget toys because he loves to fidget a lot. We can't even leave him alone; we must keep an eye on him in case he does something he's not supposed to. As days went by, my sister bought this machine called Magnetic Therapy by Sota. It was supposed to help with any type of pain or problem. In this case, it was my dad's head and cancer.

In a miracle, — we don't know what it was — if it was the machine, what he was eating or if it was what we were doing BUT the tumour on his head was starting to decrease. Thank the Lord! The machine was about £405, which is a lot of money, but it was anything for my dad. My dad was getting his beard done a few times a month, he was having his teeth brushed a few times a week; he gets cleaned with towels, and still is trying his best to have a good time. I'm so happy for him.

My Feelings

What I feel about this whole thing happening is that ... I'm so upset. It makes me sad to think about what my dad is going through. I wish that my dad was okay and that he was healthy. I just wish that I could hug him properly. I wish that he could walk and go outside. I wish that we could have the moments we used to. I wish that my dad was cured! All I wish is for my dad to be cured, happy, strong, able and stable, healthy, and finally back to my heroic dad.

My mum says it's okay to cry sometimes, so when I must, I do. It's hard to see my dad struggle. It hits me hard, but I must keep putting a smile on my face. This is not what I wished for. It's the absolute opposite. My dad is not okay. I miss his funny dance moves, his smile, his dad jokes, his car rides, his normal self.

For My Dad

I love you so much not even words can describe. You're my hope, faith, smiles, fun, and so much more. I want you to be cured and be able to do things you used to be able to do. You are my guardian. My dad, you are always there for me, so now it's my turn to do the same for you. Let me take care of you like you did for me and let me be there for you. You are my one and only Hero Dad.

Quick little update

My mum told me the news. I found out on the 13th of January that my dad had got the news of having only 1-2 months to live. I hadn't told anyone, but I had known from the very first day that they had been told this news, and I had to patch it up like I had never known. But she had finally decided to tell me for herself so I could finally let this aching out. And so, as I am writing this, my dad isn't breathing properly. He's struggling ... he's just holding on a little longer. I fear these are his last moments. My dad is going to be an angel...

Bye, my beloved daddy.

Kid's Note

Jessica

Talking about losing you will never get easier. It feels like a piece of me is missing that I will never get back. I vow to make you proud every day Papai. I miss and love you so much.

Camilla

I miss your hugs. Your little princess misses you.

Catarina

"To my daddy, my number one man, my fighter, my warrior, my tatai. I wish I could get one last hug from you, one last chance to speak to you, one last dance. I need you now and will forever need you. I still pray for you and think of you every day. I know that you are resting peacefully up there. I hope I am doing you proud. Thank you for all the beautiful memories, thank you for teaching me what true love is and thank you for teaching me that even though times are tough we shall never give up! I love you and miss you always my handsome. Until we meet again, Daddy ♥"

xxx From your biggest headache Catarina

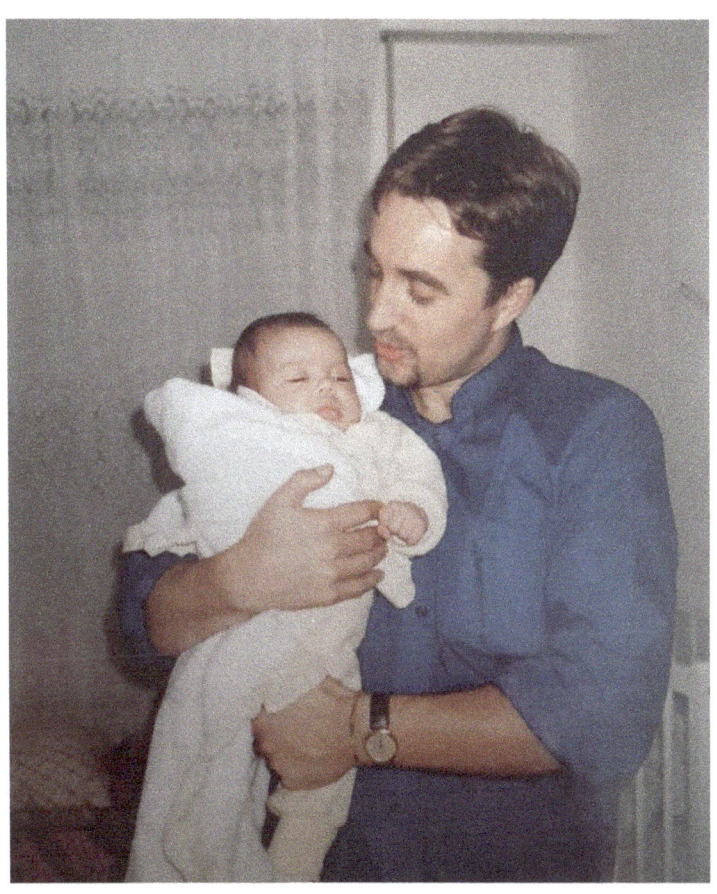

We Have a Secret 145

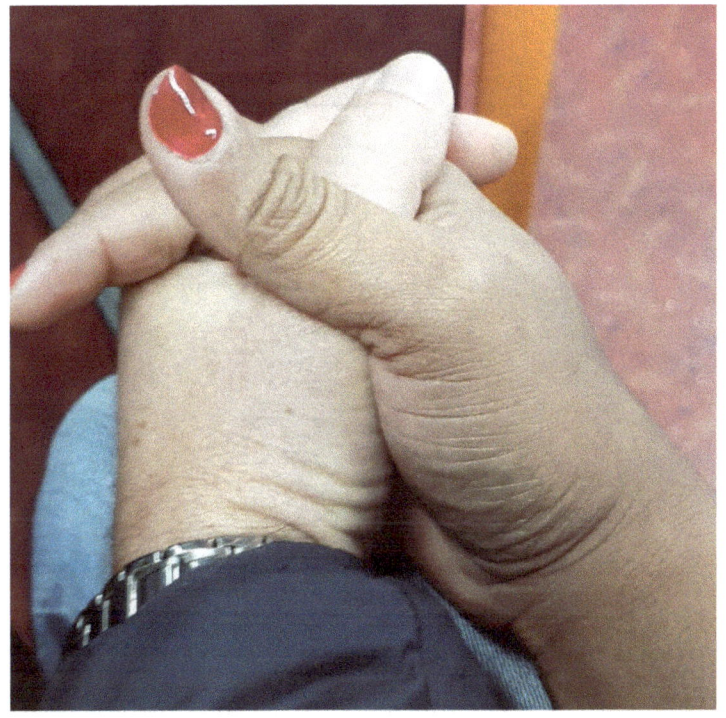

Conscious Dreams
PUBLISHING

Transforming diverse writers
into successful published authors

www.consciousdreamspublishing.com

authors@consciousdreamspublishing.com

Let's connect